BRIGHT NOTES

OF HUMAN BONDAGE
BY
W. SOMERSET
MAUGHAM

Intelligent Education

Nashville, Tennessee

BRIGHT NOTES: Of Human Bondage
www.BrightNotes.com

No part of this publication may be used or reproduced in any manner whatsoever without written permission, except in the case of brief quotations in critical articles and reviews. For permissions, contact Influence Publishers http://www.influencepublishers.com.

ISBN: 978-1-645425-30-4 (Paperback)
ISBN: 978-1-645425-31-1 (eBook)

Published in accordance with the U.S. Copyright Office Orphan Works and Mass Digitization report of the register of copyrights, June 2015.

Originally published by Monarch Press.
John F. McKinney; Robert Sobel, 1964
2019 Edition published by Influence Publishers.

Interior design by Lapiz Digital Services. Cover Design by Thinkpen Designs.

Printed in the United States of America.

Library of Congress Cataloging-in-Publication Data forthcoming.
Names: Intelligent Education
Title: BRIGHT NOTES: Of Human Bondage
Subject: STU004000 STUDY AIDS / Book Notes

CONTENTS

INTRODUCTION TO SOMERSET W. MAUGHAM

BIOGRAPHY OF W. SOMERSET MAUGHAM

William Somerset Maugham may be described with some justice as the grand old man of English letters. He was a popular playwright and novelist before many of today's crop of novelists were born, and his popularity has continued relatively undiminished down through the years. Although he has not published a new novel since 1948, he still receives royalties from his works and from motion pictures, as a result of which he is said to be one of the wealthiest men of letters of our own or any other century.

William Somerset Maugham was born on January 25, 1874. On January 25, 1964, Maugham (he never uses his first name, "William," though some of his close friends call him "Willy"), in celebrating his ninetieth birthday, could look back on a writing career of nearly seventy years, although of necessity his productivity has slackened in the last ten years. His first novel, Liza of Lambeth, was published in 1897, and is considered one of his outstanding works to this day. His first play, "Schiffbruchig," was written in German when he was eighteen years old. At one time before the First World War he had three successful comedies running at the same time on the London stage. It is estimated that his works have been published in over thirty different languages, and that over eighty million copies have been sold. His three-volume sets of 60 short stories have been purchased by one-half million people since its publication in 1962. He has earned, it is estimated, at least four million dollars from his writing and each year the royalties are still impressive. Over-all, he has published over 150 short stories, thirty plays, many travel books and essays, including works of literary criticism and commentary, and at least four important novels: *Liza of Lambeth* (1897), *The Moon and Sixpence* (1919), *The Razor's Edge* (1944), and his most noted and most important work, *Of Human Bondage* (1915).

Of Human Bondage is basically the story of W. Somerset Maugham's early life-his attempt to find himself as a man. It is thus at least partly in the tradition of the Bildungsroman, or novel of development and evolution of a young character, usually a young man, through the storm and stress of youth, adolescence, and early manhood into some reasoned and mature outlook on life. In this, *Of Human Bondage* participates in the great tradition of European literature of the nineteenth and twentieth centuries. Such novels as Goethe's *The Sorrows of Young Werther*, Dicken's *David Copperfield*, Meredith's *The Ordeal of Richard Faverel*, Samuel Butler's *The Way of All Flesh*, and that work which is perhaps most widely read in our time, Joyce's *A Portrait of the Artist as a Young Man*-these are stories of the development of a young person through a period of doubt, spiritual torment, and often physical poverty and degradation. Nor do such works always end in a mature and serene outlook, as witness the novels of Goethe and Meredith which have been cited. But *Of Human Bondage*, a partly autobiographical work, has large elements of Maugham's own early experiences in it, and ends on a relatively serene note. Mr. Maugham has himself admitted to John Beavan, the English editor and critic, that the novel was "an autobiographical book," and that it did reflect the suffering of his early life. However, the book is not entirely objective fact, and the best and most accurate statement one can make about it is that while Philip Carey is not W. Somerset Maugham as a young man, he partakes of many elements of Maugham's character and experiences.

Indeed, Maugham spoke many years after completing the work as if he was compelled to write it as a kind of purgation of early and unhappy experiences. He said to John Beavan: "The book did for me what I wanted, and when it was issued to the world... I found myself free forever of those pains and unhappy recollections. I put into it everything I knew and, having at last finished it, prepared to make a new start."

W. Somerset Maugham was born in Paris, where his father was a well-known English solicitor-a lawyer who did not actually practice in the superior courts of England but who had earned a good amount of money from his profession, so that the Maughams were well-off financially. His father was at the time of the author's birth serving as counselor to the British Embassy in Paris. Maugham's mother was noted as a beautiful woman, as may be seen from the picture of her which hangs to this day in Maugham's home. His forefathers were important in London society, and his mother also in Paris society, which accounts in part both for Maugham's cosmopolitanism and his knowledge of the higher levels of English and French society.

The rather international upbringing together with an education conducted both in English and French to the point that English was really his second language as a youth, had its advantages for him, but at the same time led to difficulties. Maugham was orphaned at an early age; both his mother and father (in reverse order from Philip Carey's loss in *Of Human*

Bondage) became ill and were both dead by the time he was ten. While Mugham had five brothers, the eldest of whom took over his father's Paris legal work, there was no home for him in Paris, and therefore Maugham, at ten, was taken under the charge of his uncle, the Anglican vicar at All Saint's Church in Whitstable. His uncle was stern and puritanical, and he became a model for Uncle William in *Of Human Bondage*. The author was not a healthy child; he had tuberculosis as a boy and, while he did not have a clubfoot like Philip Carey, he had an obvious physical defect, for he had then and has to this day a stammer which makes conversation occasionally difficult for him.

As did his most famous character Philip Carey, the author studied medicine. He was a "perpetual student" at St. Thomas' Medical School, and he did share the life of the slum dwellers in London's East End where he "led sixty-three babies into the world."

Much has been made of Maugham's poverty during his time as a medical student, obviously reflecting the plight of Philip Carey in the novel. But actually, he did have enough to live on, unlike Philip. As the playwright S. N. Behrman wrote: "He always had enough to live on just this side of poverty-a vast difference."

Poverty was a threat to W. Somerset Maugham for about a decade after he completed his medical education and decided not to devote his life to medicine but instead to pursue a career in literature. Initially, he earned barely enough to survive: an amount equal to only a few hundred dollars a year. When he attained his first success, it was as a playwright, rather than as a novelist. Today, most of his current readers have never seen even one of his plays, and it is clear that his ultimate reputation will stand or fall on the basis of his achievement as a writer of fiction.

For the last half-century W. Somerset Maugham has tasted life as a connoisseur: one who knows, and one who is interested in quality of life for its own sake-the quality of each moment. He is a collector of great art; he has traveled to every part of the globe; he has been the friend of many well-known people, including Sir Winston Churchill, Charlie Chaplin, and the Duke and Duchess of Windsor. He lives in a luxurious villa overlooking the Mediterranean Sea at Cap Ferrat. He has received the praise of whole nations, and his weekly mail averages from 400 to 500 letters from persons (mostly young people) who write to say how much they enjoyed his novels or to comment on the values they received from his work. For years, Mugham answered all of his correspondence. He was made a "Companion of Honor" by Queen Elizabeth II in 1953, and he holds the French Legion of Honor decoration.

Because of his success W. Somerset Maugham has been, or has professed to be, entirely independent of concern for the critics of his work. He has followed a similar pattern in most of his novels and in many of his short stories. Undoubtedly *Of Human Bondage* is his most famous work, and to most readers and critics it is his best. But he prefers *Cakes and Ale*, a work in which he severely criticized Hugh Walpole, the English novelist, and caricatured Thomas Hardy, the late nineteenth - and early twentieth-century British poet and novelist. He found *Cakes and Ale* an enjoyable task, and perhaps that is why his memory of it is so pleasant. On the other hand, *Of Human Bondage* was written in blood, sweat, and tears. He writes that the latter is a kind of book "that an author can only write once. After all, he has only one life."

At ninety, W. Somerset Maugham is approaching the end of that life. His days of writing are over, though there has been at least one suggestion that he has a book, again autobiographical in nature, to give the world before he is called from it. At his eighty-fifth birthday celebration he told his friends that he would not write for the public again. He said that a "writer's work must come from inside himself. He must mingle with life, must be immersed in life-and I am a stranger in the world today." He had been creative in his youth and through his maturity, but now that he is old he is ready to hand the pen over to younger men. Of course young writers have not waited to receive Maugham's abdication, for they have been imitating and asking advice from him for close to a half-century.

But W. Somerset Maugham has not given advice very easily. He has remained aloof from literary fashions and fashion plates, and apparently he wants each writer to express himself, and not to fit himself into a mold created by someone else. He does encourage young writers through a prize which he offers to writers under 35 who want to travel to broaden their outlook on life.

Maugham might best be described as a conservative in politics and an agnostic in religious outlook. The term "conservative" is to be taken in a broad sense with regard to Maugham's probable political orientation, for he has seen the government of England change considerably in the twentieth century, and with it the nature and quality of English life. He is one of the few living men who can remember when young writers, considered unstarts at the time-such men as George Bernard Shaw and H. G. Wells-were actively engaged in a struggle to improve the lot of the common man.

But while Maugham has great concern and feeling for the common man in his novels, especially in *Of Human Bondage*, as well as for the uncommon man, such as Strickland in *The Moon and Sixpence*, he seems to be a skeptic as far as his expectation of great improvement in the life of ordinary men is concerned. As a trained physician who practiced obstetrics among the poor, and as a keen observer of life, Maugham evidenced much personal humanity and charity. But he seems to posit certain inescapable conditions in life, which lead ordinary men and women to great suffering and misery. For Maugham, then, the kind of amelioration of man's lot in this world through such schemes of political improvement, such as the Fabian Socialism of Shaw, is not possible. Thus he seems to incline by temperament to conservatism, if by that is meant a perception that there are some things in the structure of society which cannot and should not be changed.

With regard to religion, the author has sought the beliefs which could sustain him but to this day does not seem to have found them. The relationship of his religious doubts to the career of Philip Carey is not an absolutely parallel one, but the reader may imagine that he went through the same struggle with his conscience as did Philip and that he has never quite finished the struggle. He wants to believe in something outside himself-a power not ourselves which makes for righteousness-but he cannot. But the lack of a firm religious belief does not seem to have turned Maugham to despair. He has been able to formulate a pattern of personal ideals and commitments which have governed his life. But it is life for this world, not for the next.

As this negative attitude toward religion reflects the life of W. Somerset Maugham, so it reflects the life of Philip Carey in *Of Human Bondage*. Philip loses one illusion after another, until he comes to believe in the utter meaninglessness of life, and there is much concern with whether the positive ending of the work erases the negative ideas proposed. The question in this regard seems to be whether Philip's realization of the vacuity of his life also allows him to realize that the emptiness came from within as well as from the environment in which he found himself. When Philip settles down with Sally, is this an admission that he was wrong and that life does have a meaning after all? Philip has always represented the man alone in the vast company of society, the alienated man, and his final rejection of far-away places and his preference for a home by the sea seem to indicate some acceptance of the values which most men accept. Philip's clubfoot had indicated his distinction and independence, as well as his isolation-that which set him apart-but when Sally loves him in spite of the deformity, may she be said to be bringing him back to humanity? These are questions which must be explored in the reading of the work.

It has commonly been observed that *Of Human Bondage* is W. Somerset Maugham's only concession to the public. This means that in giving so completely of himself, in baring his soul so much, he has not lived up to the artistic detachment demanded of the great novelist and artists in general. He does put himself into the work, in many places; this cannot be denied. But is this a defect? Some critics have observed that it is ironic that this novel has become more famous than any other work of the author, despite the fact that it is the least "detached" from the author's own life.

Fortunately, we have the author's own account of his theory of fiction as it applies to *Of Human Bondage*. On April 20, 1946, on the occasion of a ceremony at the U. S. Library of Congress in which Maugham presented the original manuscript of *Of Human Bondage* to that Library as a token of the mutual cooperation of Great Britain and the United States during the Second World War, the author said to his audience, speaking specifically of *Of Human Bondage*:

I suggest to you that it is enough for a novelist to be a good novelist. It is unnecessary for him to be a prophet, a preacher, a politician or leader of thought. Fiction is an art and the purpose of art it to please. If in many quarters this is not acknowledged I can only suppose it is because of the unfortunate impression so widely held that there is something shameful in pleasure.

But all pleasure is good. Only some pleasures have mischievous consequences and it is better to eschew them. And of course there are intelligent pleasures and unintelligent pleasures. I venture to put the reading of a good novel amongst the most intelligent pleasures that man can enjoy.*

Art, for him, must entertain. It may also be elevating or instructive, or both, but if it does not yield some measures of pleasure and entertainment, it is not really art.

The meaning of art, in Maugham's view, must not be so deeply hidden that the reader or viewer will have to wrack his brain searching for it. Art is meant to please. The artist himself may undergo torment during the creative process, as Philip Carey discovers in the world of the Paris art students, or as we see in the character of Strickland in *The Moon and Sixpence*. In fact, the demands of artistic creation are too much for most people (Fanny Price's suicide illustrates this point well in *Of Human Bondage*). But while the artist may undergo torment during the creative process-is likely so to suffer, for suffering is

---

* *"Of Human Bondage*, With a Digression on the Art of Fiction." "Address by W. Somerset Maugham, published by U.S. Government Printing Office, April, 1946.

an aspect of life and the artist attempts to tell the truth about life-his work must be the occasion of pleasure for the majority of readers or viewers.

If we accept the idea that art is meant to please there are obviously many reasons why the books of W. Somerset Maugham have delighted millions over the years. The style of his writing is simple and unaffected. While he does not over-use elaborate words and phrases when simple ones will do as well, he is at the same time a demanding writer, for he takes it for granted that his audience will be acquainted with his references to artists and politicians and novelists. And in order to maintain verisimilitude (the appearance of historical accuracy with regard to the details of his writing), for he is, after all, in *Of Human Bondage* writing of England within a rather limited social milieu at the end of the nineteenth century, Maugham uses many words and phrases which are familiar to the English reader but which the American reader may not recognize. These are identified or defined in the Glossary below in the present study guide. In short, he expects a reasonably well-educated reader.

The author is also well known for the pacing of his work. This means that he will introduce valleys and hills in his writing which will either speed up or slow down the reader. And there are periods of flatlands, too. He is a master of suspense, and he understands people and circumstances so well that there is seldom a pat ending; instead, there is usually new information provided from chapter to chapter which will direct the reader onward and stimulate his interest in the story. Maugham has a remarkable understanding of human nature, and sees good even in the worst of men, and evil, or potential evil, even in the best. To him, most life situations are neither black nor white, but rather of varying shades of grey, from an ethical point of view. He is able to give dimension to all of his characters this way, and most of his characters, even the evil genius Strickland in The Moon and Sixpence, are believable in terms of their truthfulness to life.

Further, there is continuity in Maugham's work; each scene is united with that which precedes and that which follows it. Thus when Philip receives the solace of Thorpe Athelny's friendship after his agonizing experience with Mildred Rogers, there is set up a continuity of relationship which is going to result in Philip's marriage to Athelny's daughter. This continuity is established with ease and subtlety, as a dramatist would establish continuity in a play.

W. Somerset Maugham, in *The Summing Up*, has summarized his own life. He says that he does not regret the life that he has led, and gives the impression that if he had to live all over again he would not wish his life to be different. So that, all things considered, his own life seems to have settled into a final pattern of relative serenity, much as Philip Carey's life does, or gives promise of doing, at the conclusion of *Of Human Bondage*.

He is not concerned, he says, with what contemporary critics say about his work, and he will not venture to guess what posterity will award him as an ultimate place in the world of letters. At a ninetieth birthday celebration he said, "Let posterity choose, I have done my work." The work which he found to do was to write fiction, and he became one of the most popular writers in the world. According to his own standards, he has succeeded-and his standards have been very high.

At ninety W. Somerset Maugham has given up most of the activities which were so much a part of his life before. He was formerly a dedicated bridge player, but now has given the game up because his eyesight is so bad. He is also rather deaf. But the reason for his long life may be due to his previous medical training-for he has been his own doctor-and because he has lived a life of moderation, finally following the key Greek maxim, "Nothing in excess," which his hero, Philip Carey, failed to follow, hence leading him into great difficulties in his youth.

Some five years ago, John Beavan noted that Maugham is given to fainting spells. "Darkness descends upon him from time to time, and he knows nothing more until he regains consciousness." To this the author has said with an air of resignation, "Someday I shall not." On the day that he does not wake, W. Somerset Maugham will leave behind him an enduring testament in English literature, a literary testament of which *Of Human Bondage* is, it is generally conceded by critics and readers, the greatest part.

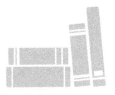

OF HUMAN BONDAGE

PART ONE

INTRODUCTION: CHAPTERS 1 AND 2

The opening scene in *Of Human Bondage* is set in a fashionable home in England in the latter half of the nineteenth century. The presence of servants and the mention of large living quarters are indications that the family living there is rather wealthy, or at least comfortably well-off. The second paragraph, and the first dialogue in the novel, introduces the hero and central character of the work, Philip Carey, who is, when we first meet him, a seven-year-old boy. His nurse wakes him and takes him to his sick mother. The atmosphere of illness fills the room, and the first cause of the sorrow is shown to be a still-born child who lies under a towel away from his mother in another corner of the room. The mother has obviously suffered greatly in the delivery of the baby, and she now pulls her living son, Philip, to her and nestles him at her side.

Comment: The author has subtly suggested the over-all viewpoint of this work in the introductory scene, and he offers a memorable picture of the dead infant, the mother dying in childbirth, and the sleeping elder son, Philip, as they gather together in the gloom that settles in the room. The author's descriptive powers dominate here, and there are only two brief sentences from the mother, both impressive and important for the development of the character of Philip: "Are you sleepy, darling?" shows the great love of the mother for her son, especially as he is living and the new infant is dead. Her second plea to the doctor, "Oh, don't take him away yet," becomes more meaningful when the reader is aware that it is a hint of the revelation of the mother's own desperate condition. She is grasping for the only thing she has left in the world: Philip.

As the doctor takes the living boy away from his mother her actions are more expressive than words could possibly be, and this illustrates what may be called the technique of drama, for, as has been pointed out, Maugham succeeded as a dramatist as well as a novelist. Her kiss and caress of the child, especially considering Philip's physical defect of his legs, are more meaningful than a scream of anguish. Her sobs as she fondles the boy's foot and her inability to express her sorrow add much reason to the mood of the moment. The reader does not know the exact reason for her tears over Philip; this will become clear later. But he does realize that this is a sorrowful situation, as though the mother's tears, repressed for a long time, were flowing uncontrollably and without her consent.

The second scene in Chapter I is in the corner of the same room where the doctor views the body of the dead infant, a boy. The doctor's comment to his nurse, "I don't think there's anything I can do just now," is a hint of his inability to do anything ever to save Mrs. Carey. He leaves the room dejectedly, aware of the limitations of medicine. The question which the nurse asks regarding Mrs. Carey's brother-in-law helps to emphasize the point that her condition is most grave. The nurse seems concerned to get the living son away from this atmosphere of death, and death it will be, we are finally assured, as the doctor shakes his head to the nurse's question: "D'you think Mrs. Carey will get over it, sir?"

Comment: It is important to realize that the first chapter sets much of the mood of this novel, as it pucks a child out of the world of comfort and maternal love into a society where as an orphan he will never again feel the same scene of security, of belonging and being wanted. The author's plot shows itself at the outset to be impressive in its simplicity, while his dialogue is quite direct and he allows the reader to ponder and to discover his own emotional response to the situation. A second point to note is the way Mr. Maugham interweaves words like "grey" and "dull" and also his references to heavy clouds and rawness in the air. All of these images set the atmosphere of gloom in external nature and, important, reflect the sadness in the minds of the participants in the scene. It is interesting that the first chapter demonstrates Maugham's background as a playwright, a craft in which he ex-celled and won much praise before he returned to the writing of the novel just before 1920. The entire opening chapter of *Of Human Bondage* might be acted on the stage, and it is easy to see that

the characters say more with their actions than with their words. The doctor's negative nod at the end of this chapter is more grave than if he had tearfully announced, "No, she will die!"

In the second chapter the author also introduces two important scenes which allow the reader insight into Philip Carey's emotions. The first lines present Philip in a normal boy's activity, playing "cowboys and Indians" in a parlor of his mother's friend. There he is discovered by his nurse Emma, who destroys his make-believe cave and brings him back to reality. Philip's first question is quite normal for a boy away from home, and he is pleased when he finds that he will be going back now. An example of the child's thinking is his reference to the nurse's new dress, and the question startles her, for she anticipated some remark about his mother. Finally, the nurse has to remind him of his mother, and the answer, "Oh, I forget. How is mamma?" allows the nurse to introduce the words she has prepared. She is subtle and perhaps religiously reflective as she refers to the deceased mother as "quite well and happy." But when the boy does not comprehend her meaning, she must be more direct: "Your mamma's gone away. You won't see her anymore." Still, the meaning is unknown to the child, and his question "Why Not?" is answered by, "Your mama's in heaven." The deluge of tears which closes this scene and the boy's lack of understanding as to why he is crying are points of **irony** in the author's design of the work. He is showing the reader something of the mentality of a young child and emphasizing the fact that emotions of this type are unknown to children because they cannot comprehend the thought of death.

The scene which follows in Chapter 2 involves the tearful goodbyes to Miss Watkin, who has been caring for him, and to her friends. At first Philip does not want them to see that he has been crying, but somehow he senses that they will be sorry for him and that the situation offers him a chance to take the spotlight in an adult world. He seems to enjoy the prestige of suffering, although he was not able to feel genuinely his mother's death. Philip enjoys the condolence and consideration of the women and offers a pretense of bravery when he announces: "I've got to get home," words uttered with the dedication of a soldier returning to his post on the battlefield. He leaves the room, but before he leaves the house both he and the reader are told important details which will govern their emotions throughout the rest of the novel. When Philip finally hears the word "dead" applied to his mother, and when the reader is told that the boy has a clubfoot, all the essential scars of his life are known. The untimely death of his parents, plus the physical defect of the clubfoot, are psychic scars which are to condition Philip's life, both consciously and unconsciously.

It is important to emphasize Philip's reaction as he overhears the adults speaking about him on two occasions. Each time the author allows the reader to gather important information which is required to set the dramatic situation in the novel moving. When Philip overhears Miss Watkin's lament over his mother's death and a stranger's reference to the fact that he is now an orphan as well as to the fact that he has a clubfoot, the details about the important irrational forces which condition Philip's character are complete.

SUMMARY AND CONCLUSION:

The first two chapters of *Of Human Bondage* are most important, and may be said to have the following functions:

1. They establish an atmosphere of the gloom and tragedy which will pervade much of the work until the hero, Philip, attains his final mature outlook on life.

2. The irrationality of life is stressed; there is no particular reason why Philip should have a clubfoot or why his mother should die in childbirth and leave him an orphan, but these grim things happen, and no rational explanation is indicated.

3. The helplessness of man's arts and sciences in the face of death is revealed: medicine, the calling which Philip is to pursue much later in the story, is shown to have little power to avert these senseless tragedies.

4. In short, the first two chapters reveal the author's view that life is essentially irrational and probably meaningless into the bargain, and gives just a hint that the important thing is the way in which man responds to the circumstances of life.

LIFE WITH THE VICAR: CHAPTERS 3-9

In the beginning of this section Philip meets his uncle, Mr. Carey, again, but this meeting is to be very different from their meetings in the past when Philip spent an occasional holiday with his uncle, a vicar in the Anglican Church, and with his aunt Louisa, the vicar's wife. The vicar is a man of God, but he has always seemed austere and distant to Philip, and the boy's remembrance of his uncle is not pleasant. But if the boy is awed by his uncle, the uncle is nonetheless concerned by the intrusion of the boy into his life. The vicar and his wife had been married for over thirty years without having children of their own. Philip's uncle is shown essentially a good man, although narrow and perhaps overly avaricious. He is accustomed to live a quiet and moderate life, and it becomes obvious that he did not agree with the late Mrs. Carey, Philip's mother, on the way she managed her money. It is at this time that the author gives the reader a small bit of knowledge about Philip's father also. The father had been a medical doctor-Philip's ultimate profession-of talent, but his life was cut short by blood-poisoning, a common occurrence in nineteenth-century medicine, only six months previous to the beginning of the novel. But Maugham is careful not to stress Philip's father and his fate, for it might be too much if the reader's emotions became involved with the father as well as with the dead mother and the orphaned boy. Maugham here avoids excessive appeal to the merely sentimental and pathetic.

Since Philip is quite dependent upon his nurse Emma, he naturally asks if she will be with him when he goes to live with his uncle and aunt. The negative answer is only one of the heartaches which Philip is to feel in his move from London to the country town of Blackstable, where his uncle's parish is. Philip is allowed to keep one thing belonging to each of his parents, a remembrance of them, and it is in searching for these mementos that he has a fuller realization of what his mother's death will mean to him. Of course it is not possible that he will understand completely, but the first serious consideration is there. Even so, his mind rebels against the thought of permanent separation from his mother:

...it seemed to him that his mother had just gone out for a walk. She would be in presently and would come upstairs to have nursery tea with him. And he seemed to feel her kiss on his lips.

But Philip soon realized that his mother would not be coming, for within a few days he found himself on a train, bidding goodbye to his nurse Emma, and on his way to start a new life with his uncle the vicar and his aunt Louisa. The box is welcomed most graciously by Aunt Louisa, and he is treated with aloof kindness by his uncle, who is obviously the dominating person in his household. Since he is a man of religion he speaks of that subject quite often, and soon the young Philip knows of the religious distinctions and dissensions of the people of the area. The author takes some pains to point out the bickering which goes on within and without the Anglican Church. Yet W. Somerset Maugham does not seem to be attacking any religion or religious value: rather, he is pointing out the frailty of the ministers of God's will.

Comment: The vicar is presented as a rather interesting character study. He is extremely frugal, as indicated by the fact that he shares his daily paper with two others. He doesn't like to be contradicted on any count, and he doesn't like to loose at cards (his wife abets his pride of accomplishment by losing purposely to him). He favors an ordered life, with precise times for eating, bathing, sleeping, in fact, for everything. His own religious beliefs are so strong that he feels that every one who disagrees with him is lost to Satan. And yet, in so many ways his religious life is empty, for he has difficulty in putting his own sermons into practice. Thus we find that he is proud, self-indulgent, and arrogant in his

dealings with his wife, his sexton, and his fellow clergymen. Yet in spite of his faults one can see some good qualities in him.

Certainly his wife Louisa sees many good things in him. She has been his wife for over thirty years and understands his every whim and caprice. The simplicity of her love for him is demonstrated by the fact that she accepts his ill humor and his most serene joy without question. The reader might feel that she should rebel against him when he is selfish or cross, but that is something she would never do. Her acceptance of the religious and social values of the day would certainly prohibit it, but more than the idea of conformity is found here. It is essentially a deep and generous love on her part which balances the negative points of her husband.

Philip's relationship with his aunt soon turns to a sincere love on the part of both of them, but the boy's relationship with his uncle is always something shy of love. It is true that after a short time at the parsonage Philip offers his hand as a gesture of trust and affection as the uncle and he walk to services, but within a short time there is a break in that affection, and for a long time afterward Philip views his uncle with less affection and more arrogance. In this respect the eighth chapter presents a turning point in the relations of the boy to his uncle. Philip was always a quiet, shy boy, and after his mother's death he was never more happy than when alone. In this situation we find the boy playing on the kitchen floor on a Sunday. He has some bricks and while playing them he disturbs his uncle's regular Sunday nap. The uncle, who was already peeved by the church sexton, now takes his anger out on the boy and constantly refers to the incident during the day. Yet, Philip does not protest, for he seems to realize that his uncle is incapable of being moved by any of his bitter words. But he does realize that his aunt Louisa is capable of being hurt, since it is she who has a genuine love and concern for him. Thus when she tries to explain her husband's behavior and asks him, "Don't you love me at all?" he screams at her "I hate you. I wish you were dead."

Aunt Louisa's reactions at his declaration are only quiet sobs and then flowing tears, and it is only when Philip realizes that she truly loves him that he also realizes how dependent he is on her as the only person who really loves him in all the world. His kiss on her tear-stained cheek is a sign that all the strangeness between them has disappeared.

After the unfortunate incident with his uncle noted above, Philip is relegated to the library on the subsequent Sunday afternoon to memorize part of the church service for that day. The boy's efforts are thwarted by fear of failure, but his sadness is turned to joy by a fortunate suggestion made by his aunt that he be allowed to use the time to browse through some pictures of the Holy Land in a magazine. The pictures intrigue Philip and whet his appetite for more, and thus in an unusual way Philip is introduced to the world of art, a world in which he was to find himself interested and also talented, and one which was to shape events in his life some ten years later. Of course the picture books also have words in them, and the words also stimulated Philip, so much so that he eagerly sought other works which promised him romance and adventure and a release from a world which was becoming too complex for an orphan with a clubfoot.

Philip's great joy in reading and painting was a very fortunate point in his life, for he was able to find satisfaction without other playmates of his age. It was not that playmates were not available, but the vicar, Mr. Carey, thought that the neighbor's children were too rough for him. Yet, in spite of the vicar's good intentions, his shielding of Philip was to have a negative effect on the boy's personality. It was to hurt the boy's development in his later relations with boys in school and with men and women in the world. And it was at this time that his uncle chose to start him on his schoolboy career in King's School, where it was expected that he might follow Mr. Carey in the service of the church.

Certainly this expectation was not strong in Philip's mind as he set out for school, but he accepted the situation with the sense of adventure which influences every boy of his age. It was a step which was to mark the end of adolescence and the beginning of maturity for him.

Comment: In these chapters, some idea of W. Somerset's apparent views on the formal Anglican religion of the end of the nineteenth century and the beginning of the twentieth are made clear. The stage is set for Philip's ultimate loss of religious faith and his refusal to follow his uncle and to be ordained a clergyman. By the dryness, by the spiritual and emotional sterility demonstrated by Philip's uncle, Philip is conditioned; in modern psychological terminology, one might say that Philip is a child starved for affection, and that he comes to identify a person - the vicar, his uncle - with a set of beliefs, the Christian religion. And because his uncle, a distinctly fallible human being, cannot rise to his need and be as a father to Philip, the boy sees the religion of his uncle as empty and without meaning. But in these early chapters, little of these thoughts intrude themselves into Philip's thoughts.

SUMMARY AND CONCLUSION:

Chapters 3 through 9 have the following purposes:

1. They show Philip's gradually developing awareness of himself and his surroundings. He is nine years old - the year, by the way, is 1885 when he comes to the vicar's house - and therefore is presented as two years younger than Maugham, which is perhaps symbolic of Maugham's wish not to make Philip entirely an autobiographical character.

2. These chapters call into question the vicar's religious faith, and tend to undercut it by showing that the vicar, despite his profession, is not able to show that true charity which Philip's needs require.

3. Daily life in a vicarage in the English countryside is presented with somewhat of a satirical intent, for it is by no means idyllic.

4. The character of Philip's aunt is developed, and she is shown to be essentially a good woman, who will have much influence on Philip's early development, although Philip ultimately will come to pity her and to fall away from her rather unthinking piety.

LIFE AT SCHOOL: CHAPTERS 10-22

Life at King's School at Tercanbury was an opening to an entirely new world for Philip Carey, and he found that it was not designed especially for his liking. After his initial enthusiasm for school (since it would allow him to get away from domination of his uncle), he became fearful of it. He feared strangers who might not accept him because of his clubfoot. He resented strangers who would accept him because of it. Since his deformity had made him unusually shy and awkward, and because he lived with it every day, he thought that it would be something which others would not be able to accept.

After Philip is swept up and away from his uncle by the head-master Mr. Watson, the boy is made aware of his loneliness in his new surroundings. Philip had always been sensitive and withdrawn because of his limp, and now lodged with other boys of his own age who were not as subtle as adults, he is made to feel incompetent and inferior. He cannot compete with them on the athletic field and his financial situation forbids him many of their activities. And since he is not strong nor sociable he is soon made the butt of the school bully. Yet, it is this situation which gives the reader some insight into the character of Philip, for there is a quality revealed which will remain with the boy throughout his life. Philip is constantly attacked by the bully Singer, and on the occasion the latter demands to see Philip's deformed foot. Of course Philip refuses, but this gives Singer the opportunity to show his physical superiority and so he wrenches Philip's arm. After suffering intense pain Philip gives in and suffers the humiliation which the bully gives. But Philip's reaction is not in tears, nor in anger, for he believes it is only a bad dream that will be over in the morning, and that with the new day he will be home and happy with his mother. It is in dreams that he finds much of his solace in his youth, and it is dreams which direct his steps toward the sea in his later life.

But life at school is not all bad. Philip does discover some sympathy in the behavior of Mr. Rice, a teacher, and he does find success in his studies. After a time his deformity is accepted, or rather ignored, and he is allowed to join the boys in their non-athletic endeavors. His efforts to find friends is quite noble and he will take the risks of offending the instructors to gain the acclaim of the crowd. But his efforts are frustrated when he and Singer are caught playing "nibs," for he is not punished while Singer is. It is a situation which Philip would like to see reversed, but the headmaster would not "hit a cripple." Thus Philip is again left out of the boys' activity altogether, and as the years progress at school Philip moves more and more into himself. He becomes a dreamer, and the dream is often of his former life in London with his father and mother.

The next two years brought academic success to Philip, and he had a number of plaques and scrolls to indicate his proficiency in various subjects. But his success in studies did not bring social acceptance. Many students let it be known that they did not want to compete with him since he was crippled. In hiding their own incompetence or laziness they said, "After all, it's jolly easy for him to get prizes...there's nothing he can do but swat." Thus Philip found himself still alone, and he was alone at a particularly trying time. His "growing pains" were primarily emotional and they grew out of his social situation. He needed love, and if not that, at least companionship, but all seemed to be denied to him.

An example of this need is found in his lie to Luard when the other boy breaks Philip's pen-holder. Philip's declaration that it was his mother's is meant only to solicit pity from the other boy. It is all a pose, and an awkward one at that, as Philip soon realizes. But it not unique in Philip's history, for he felt the same elevation in sorrow and pity when his mother died and he became the center of attraction at Miss Watkin's house at a date much earlier in his life.

Chapter 14 finds Philip in the throbs of his most vital religious experience. He had been educated in the home of religious people, and he had accepted the Anglican faith as it had been handed to him. Now he begins to feel a more genuine need for participating in his faith, and thus he turns to the Bible for its strength and consolation. He runs across the lesson that faith can move mountains and feels that he might be able to apply that message to his own life and particularly to cure his clubfoot. He has great faith in religion as a healing force and begins a period of great fasting and mortification, with the avowed intention and expectation that he will be cured miraculously. His imagination even finds him returning to school without his limp and becoming an outstanding athlete. It can all come true, he thinks, if only I have faith. He finds encouragement in the religious assurance of his uncle, the vicar, but when the miracle doesn't occur Philip is greatly disappointed. Yet with the optimism of youth he determines to begin his plan anew, only to encounter the same result again. Yet the second defeat is not as much of a jolt as the first. Philip seems to have suspected it all along, as his remark that "I suppose no one ever has faith enough" indicates. Such faith and religious values begin to take on the aura of a fairy tale, and from this time until much later in his life religion will not have the impact it formerly had.

When he was thirteen Philip Carey left the preparatory school and moved over to the senior division at King's School. It was here that he was to grow out of adolescence toward maturity, and he found himself at the school when it was going through the greatest changes in its history. There were new ideas taking over in education and there were many members of the old guard at King's School who were fighting them. The school was now under the direction of a dynamic person, Mr. Perkins, who was ready to sweep some of the cobwebs out of the classroom. In this respect it seems appropriate to say that W. Somerset Maugham, himself, is in agreement with the educational reform of the age.

In chapter 16 the author presents the contrast between Mr. Perkins, who represents the modern movement in education, and Mr. Gordon, who is dead set against change. The latter's method of teaching relies upon the harsh word and the hard stick, and his military approach frustrates and frightens young Philip. In contrast, when Mr. Perkins takes over the class occasionally, Philip is able to express himself without fear of reproach, and because he has great ability, he excels. On one particular occasion Mr. Gordon is particularly severe with Philip, and after he abuses him with "Blockhead! Blockhead! Blockhead! Clubfooted Blockhead!" the teacher sends the student to the headmaster for punishment. But when Philip confronts Mr. Perkins the punishment is not severe, as the headmaster befriends the boy and opens new worlds of knowledge for him.

As the years go by Philip finds school life more bearable. He is never a popular boy, but he is in the upper grades now and is no longer the physical butt of the bully. The studies are less demanding here, and with the aid of crib sheets which were passed from year to year there is no great need to prepare homework or for examinations. Mr. Maugham seems to emphasize the tendency to cheat in students, and his off-hand acceptance of it is not to condone it. He seems to be saying that this is one way many students prepare for life - by cheating. Maugham also is criticizing Mr. Weeks for his laxity and boredom, and particularly for the effect which his attitude has on the students. In one of the most ironic statements in the book Mr. Weeks comments that he has no faith in examinations as the boys never seem to do as well in them as in class recitation.

Fortunately, the boys are rescued from Mr. Weeks in the Upper Third as they progress up the scholastic ladder. On the next rung they fell into the hands of Mr. Turner, in whose hands their academic course was straightened. In this course Philip was much happier, and as his spirit brightened he found new meaning in life and particularly in the world of nature about him. He also began to experience a renewed need for religion in his life after he had allowed it to fade after his disappointment regarding his clubfoot. He has great respect and admiration for Mr. Perkins and confides in him the thoughts which his uncle and aunt have regarding Philip's religious vocation. Under the influence of Mr. Perkins his religious fervor is strengthened and Philip soon imagines that he is already ordained in the Anglican Church, living in complete subjection to the will of God. In the throbs of this religious fervor he dreams of himself on the day of ordination as he limps through the ceremony, offering his physical deformity as sacrifice to the will of God.

But just as Philip's religious fervor had quickly blossomed, so it quickly wilted, and he was soon in the same spirit of religious indifference which he had known previously. And since he could not find an outlet in athletics and through friendship with the other boys, Philip continues to emphasize his studies. His success as a student offers him a feeling of superiority and he found it difficult"...to hide his contempt for his companion's stupidity." Because he was witty he often criticized his fellow students, and their reaction only made him more unpopular and alone. Philip was caught between two evils: he had to find some way to express himself and his studies were the only possibility; but the excellence in his studies separated him from the other boys. He would gladly exchange places with the dumbest boy in the class if only the others would accept him.

Then, to his great surprise and joy, someone came into his life who offered the kindness and friendship and road to acceptance which Philip so desperately needed. He is befriended by one of the most popular boys at school and as such he is accepted into the society of the others. His friend is named Rose, and soon there grows a strong friendship between them, so much so that Philip is disappointed when he has to go home for vacation. Thus, his stay at home is difficult since he longs to get back to Rose, and he is only too happy to leave on the train when it is time. He looks forward eagerly to meet Rose at the station, but his efforts are frustrated when he realizes that his friend was not as anxious to see him.

It is in this situation that Philip shows another trait in his character which is to cause him great pain as he struggles through life. He becomes jealous over Rose's friendship and activity with other boys, and this reaction causes him to imagine situations which do not exist and to exaggerate those which do. He feels similarly possessive about people in his later life, and as such it seems an outgrowth of his own sense of inferiority. He has so little affection in this world that he wants to possess Rose all to himself.

At this time illness comes to make his relationship with Rose all the more difficult. Philip has scarlet fever, and he is confined and quarantined over the Easter vacation and through the beginning of the summer. As such he does not return to class until the term is half finished. He is most anxious to meet Rose again and to resume their friendship, but he soon realizes that a few months is a long time to be away, and when he returns he is hardly acknowledged by Rose. Philip is crushed. Because he is so sensitive his emotions are difficult to control, and within a short time he is an enemy of his former friend, and an outcast again. Again, Philip finds solace in his assumed superior attitude, and he multiplies his own agony by being difficult with the other boys. He acts in a way which is the opposite of his real feelings, so much so that he hardly realizes what he says. A very poignant example of this occurs when Rose does make an effort to be friendly, but the boy is cut down by Philip's tart words: "You bore me." The words were hardly out of his mouth when he wanted to recall them, but his pride wouldn't allow him to do so. Thus the relations between the two former friends are strained beyond repair, and aside from its immediate effect of making Philip (and probably Rose) miserable, it set up a series of events which were to see Philip become so miserable that he became obsessed with the idea of leaving school.

The desire for freedom from school is a normal desire in a teenage boy, but in Philip's case it was more intense because it was born of frustration. After his alienation from Rose he had no purpose in life and soon his academic standing dropped. But Philip did not seem to care. He found some outlet in his talent for drawing, but this was aimless and repetitious, and soon he was questioned by the headmaster as to what the trouble was. The trouble was that Philip was bored and miserable, but he could not tell that to Mr. Perkins. In a memorable meeting between these two, Mr. Perkins tells Philip of the beauty of a life devoted to God and the church through scholarship, and, under the influence of his teacher, Philip almost breaks down to confess his sorrow and sadness. Yet there is something so stubborn and rebellious in him that he will not allow himself to repent. Thus he leaves Mr. Perkins without a change in his attitude, and once he is away from the teacher's impressive words regarding the church he feels that he can view the life of a pastor much more objectively. He sees the loneliness of the church; he accents the hypocrisy of ministers he has known, particularly of his own uncle. He makes up his mind that he will not enter into the church and that he must leave school.

But before Philip Carey does finally exit from the doors of King's School he still has some formidable problems to overcome. His uncle and aunt are opposed to his leaving, and Mr. Perkins feels that he will be throwing away a fine career. But Philip is obsessed with the idea of leaving, and of going to Germany to learn the ways of the world. Point by point he beats down (or ignores) the arguments of his uncle, aunt, and Mr. Perkins, until they agree to his withdrawal from school. But Philip finds his victory over adults is not as sweet as he had thought. In another memorable scene with Mr. Perkins he realizes the validity of the teacher's argument to stay, but Philip is too far committed in his own pride to recant now. He is afraid of the taunts which would be directed at him by his classmates if he gave in to the wisdom of adults and sacrificed his own will.

The conclusion of chapter 21 finds Philip ready to leave King's School. He had won! He was going to Germany. He would be away from the regimen and religion of the school; he was free from the callous remarks of his fellow students who did not understand him. And yet the freedom which he had so long sought now brought him new fears: "He wondered whether he had done right. He was dissatisfied with himself and with all his circumstances. He asked himself dully whether whenever you get your way you wished afterward that you hadn't."

Comment: These school scenes are of great historical and sociological interest, as well as being of crucial importance in Philip's development. Remember that the King's School of Tercanbury is an English

preparatory school of the turn of the century, and that it was one of a number of educational institutions which had enormous influence in the patterning of English society. "Fagging" (hazing or the punishment of the younger boys by the older ones) was the rule, and Philip early in these chapters comes in for more than his share of such abuse. This, too, profoundly affects him, causing him to retreat into his shell - a shell which is opened, though only temporarily, by the wise and dynamic headmaster, Perkins. But generally the education provided at the school is satirized by Maugham as being barren and leading to false and empty social distinctions.

The tone of the school chapters is, by and large, satirical. Maugham examines the preparatory school as an institution, and shows certain of its more vicious elements.[*] Even Mr. Perkins, the brilliant and powerful headmaster of King's whom the other masters resent because he has "climbed above himself" socially, is presented as having at least one shortcoming: he attempts to influence Philip to become ordained, and as a matter of fact very nearly succeeds at the end in keeping Philip at the school. But Philip rebels and leaves, turning down the chance to go to Oxford and read for the Church. And, as Maugham presents the situation, it seems that he

[*] An interesting and supposedly factual essay which gives a picture of such a school in England in the 1900's is George Orwell's "Such, Such Were the Joys..." in *Orwell, A Collection of Essays* (N.Y.: Doubleday and Co., 1954), pp. 9–55.

has relatively little sympathy for what Mr. Perkins tries to do in Philip's case.

Philip's psychological scars are shown in these chapters as being deepened by the treatment he receives at the school. For while Mr. Perkins is kind to him, even as he tries to talk Philip into embracing the ministry of the Church of England, the boys and the other masters are generally less than kind, and the boys torment him because his club foot makes him "different."

Actually, the education which Philip receives at the school is largely self-education. He comes to take an independent line: with the vicar, his uncle, and finally with Mr. Perkins, over the question of ordination. Philip's final break with Mr. Perkins and the school is treated ambiguously, because, as Maugham tells us in Chapter 21 of Philip:

> "It only required a little more persuasion, just enough to save his self-respect, and Philip would have done anything that Mr. Perkins wished; but his face showed nothing of his conflicting emotions. It was placid and sullen. "I think I'd rather go, sir," he said.

A little bit more, and Philip would have slipped back, for the Church puts on its best face in the person of Mr. Perkins, a genuinely dedicated teacher and educational leader. But as Maugham presents it, Philip's ultimate welfare lies in another direction than the Church.

SUMMARY AND CONCLUSION:

Chapters 10 through 22 have the following purposes:

1. They satirize the educational theories and practices of the times - the period of the 1880s and 90s - in England.

2. They show Philip's continued development and his striking out for himself, inwardly at first, and finally in outward rebellion, against his guardian and his teachers.

3. Philip is presented at this stage as in some respects unpleasant; he is "different," as symbolized by his clubfoot, and is cruelly treated by some of the boys.

4. Philip is shown as feeling sorry for himself, as evidenced especially by the incident of the broken pen-holder.

THE GERMAN ADVENTURE: CHAPTERS 23–31

Since Philip Carey had been so determined to leave school in England, there was little which his uncle and aunt could do to prevent him. But there is concern on their part for his future and for his religious training. Thus they arrange through a friend, a Miss Wilkinson (about whom we are to hear much more later), to have Philip boarded and educated in the home of Professor and Frau Professor Erlin in Heidelberg. And it is to that famous German city that Philip travels as he escapes from the discipline of King's school. He arrives in the month of May, but to his sorrow he finds that life in his new surroundings can be just as lonely and boring as it was in England. He is lost in the culture and language and customs of the German people, and it takes him a long time to overcome his deficiency.

In the home of Frau Professor Erlin he is received hospitably by her and her family. She is quite motherly toward him, as are her two daughters, and all three are much more vital characters than Professor Erlin himself. The professor is a highly educated man, but he is not very dynamic. He is content to let his wife run the house and his life. He greets Philip with English which would have been appropriate in the time of Shakespeare, but which is not spoken in modern England. Philip also meets the other guests who are boarding at Frau Professor Erlin's, sixteen in all, and finds them to be rather a strange mixture of society. They are drawn together in Heidelberg for various reasons, but they are staying at the Erlin's because of the good food and the reasonable rent.

Philip is extremely bashful in his first associations with the Erlin family and the other guests. He is not accustomed to the company of girls at this time and he finds himself awkward and confused when he talks to them, as he is on the occasion of a walk into the country on his first night in Germany. Yet, the evening is not a total loss, for in spite of his situation Philip is awed by the beauty of the Rhine Valley when he sees it, and it inspires in him a great joy and confidence that he has taken the right step in coming to study. Thus the first day of his adventure ends with Philip commenting to himself: "By Jove, I am happy." It is a moment which seems to be Philip's first awakening to the joys of nature. He finds that he is growing up, and that he has freedom at last.

Freedom meant many things to Philip, but the most interesting of these at this time was the fact "that he need not tell any more lies." It is a remark which seems to hit at the center of Philip's own inferiority complex, and because there is no more need to lie he begins to get out from the feelings of inferiority and to start on the road to maturity. Part of this growing up is certainly Philip's exposure to new people and beliefs. His mathematics teacher proved to be quite a revelation. His name was Wharton, a fellow Englishman, whom Philip found to be lazy, fat, and very self-indulgent. Between lessons in mathematics the young boy found out something of the man's ideals and behavior. Wharton resents Philip's money, and is often tempted to be rude to the boy, but Philip is not taken in and really has compassion for the teacher. Yet Philip cannot understand many of the man's habits: he drinks excessively, his clothes and bed linen are filthy. But Wharton defends his behavior by stressing the freedom which they represent. In passing, Wharton criticizes many things formerly sacred to Philip, such as the English people themselves, for they are too conventional in thought and deed - and Americans are worse in his opinion. It is all very illuminating for Philip, for the values of Wharton contrast so much with the ideals of a young boy who is taught at home.

Philip also learns something of German social standards. The two girls in Erlin's home are in love with men, but the younger, Hedwig, has chosen a man above her social class. Thus she is constantly lamenting her fate and talking of love, and when Philip repeats her remark, using the words "Ich liebe dich" (I love you), she reminds him not to speak to her in such a familiar way. The **irony** here is that the German language has and the German people accept two forms for "you," the personal pronoun, and Philip does not know Hedwig well enough to use "dich" (it should be "Sie"). But the situation is all part of Philip's worldly education, and although he has no tender feelings for Hedwig he allows her to think so. It is all very flattering to her and all a lark to him.

As part of his formal education Philip also studies the great figures of German culture, notably Faust by the great German poet Goethe. Professor Erlin praises Goethe's genius to Philip and contrasts the poet with the young writers of the day. To Professor Erlin the new works were "obscene nonsense," and he attacked them with vehemence. He viewed the public's acceptance of them as representative of "the ruin of the family, the uprooting of morals, the destruction of Germany." All of this seems to stress the professor's obsession with the past and ignorance of the present, for W. Somerset Maugham notes that the man he most despises is Henrik Ibsen, who is considered today to be the father of modern drama. The composer Richard Wagner also is attacked by the professor, and the latter considers Wagner's opera Siegfried as "the greatest hoax of the nineteenth century." Again this is representative of the closed mind of Philip's teacher, and it certainly seems to be representative of the author's indictment of that attitude.

Philip's French teacher was Monsieur Ducroz, and he, too, shared the same fate of poverty and squalor as Mr. Wharton. But there the similarity ended, for Monsieur Ducroz was quiet and sober. His past was cloudy, but Philip heard of former adventures when his teacher fought with the republican forces in Italy. This puzzled Philip, but the teacher passed it off lightly to the student. This was typical of the teacher's actions, for in everything he was passive and unruffled. He always carried a refined attitude with him in the midst of his poverty. His revolutionary days were over and he may now feel that all of his efforts were worthless and that man will never want to be released from his oppression. The teacher was a man of great pride and great poverty. The former prevents him from begging to alleviate the latter. Thus, when Philip offers to pay for a great many lessons in advance to help his teacher, the boy expects some show of thanks for his generosity. But none is forthcoming at first, and it is not until the teacher has recovered his strength that he does refer to Philip's act of kindness. In a memorable scene in which Maugham's ability to project character comes out quite clearly we find Monsieur Ducroz groping for words to express his thanks. He gives it quite simply: "If it hadn't been for the money you gave me I should have starved. It was all I had to live on." Philip has learned something of the heroic from him. And something of the meaning of independence.

In the midst of his studies Philip becomes more aware of the problems of the Erlin family, notably that Fraulein Hedwig's lover had finally won over his parents to the qualities of the young girl and that they would soon be coming to visit. But the involvement with the family soon becomes incidental to Philip's involvement with a new boarder at the Erlin home. He is another Englishman named Hayward, and he presents quite a contrast to Philip in many ways. But because Hayward is a man of the world Philip soon accepts his ideas and poses, being somewhat taken by the apparent brilliance of the new arrival. However, there is a man who is staying at the house who is not as easily impressed, and who soon proves to be a foil to the grand designs and inconsistencies of Hayward. This is Weeks, an American theological student, and it seems obvious that W. Somerset Maugham introduces him as a contrast to the character of Hayward. Thus, when Hayward has thoroughly influenced Philip by his negative attitude and constant criticism of society's standards, Weeks utterly deflates the argument of Hayward with his cool logic, and in the process shows how shallow the Englishmen really is. It is not a pleasant experience for Hayward, but he asked for it with his overbearing assurance. There is a memorable scene when the three begin their discussions. One night the topic turns to Greek tragedies and Hayward shows off his wisdom with vague ideas and generalizations - and finds that Weeks is ready to pounce upon him with a far greater knowledge and understanding of the subject.

It appears that W. Somerset Maugham wants to emphasize the differences between Hayward and Weeks. Hayward might be classified as a "wandering intellectual," and he is quite impressive at first sight and upon the first meeting. But Maugham seems to be pointing out the shallowness of his ideas and the shallowness of the society which has formed him. Hayward is of the upper class of English society and he has been able to develop his interest in literature and art in general, but in the process he has become an example of malcontented sickness. He has positive values of religion, at this moment agreeing with the ideals of the Catholic Church, but his laxity is carried over to the world of the spirit and he allows his belief to fade as has his own talent. Also, he constantly judges things in a material way, referring to money almost with reverence. And most discouraging of all in the final analysis of his character is his fraudulent claim to be a man of the arts. He refers to books which he is going to write, the criticisms which will startle the age with their brilliance, but in spite of this he never finishes a work. It is almost as though Hayward were deceiving himself with his pretense of authorship and scholarship.

Weeks, on the other hand, is somewhat reserved in his opinions at first, and, as noted above, he allows his opponent to fall into a trap before he demonstrates his knowledge of the subject. Weeks is a man searching for truth in religion and in life, and he is not afraid to answer "I don't know," when that is the honest answer. But what Weeks seems to dislike most about Hayward is the pompous behavior and the faulty logic of his ideals. Weeks is able to size up Hayward early and recognizes him as the author of numerous books which will not be written. As such he is almost brutal in his appraisal of Hayward to Philip, and he tells him things which Philip will only fully comprehend years later.

All of this is quite a revelation to Philip Carey. He erroneously sides with Hayward in the arguments between the Englishman and the American, but in the scope of their dissent he receives a rather liberal education which touches on religion and ethics, art and intellectual acrobatics. At times it is rather frustrating for Philip for he has the unhappy habit of expressing himself awkwardly at times and the other two quickly cut him down to size.

Among the new points which Philip learns are the points of belief in Buddhism and Mohammedanism and he is particularly taken by Weeks' reference to Unitarianism. In his own background in England it was maintained that gentlemen are not Unitarians, and of course Philip accepted this. In a subtle piece of **irony** Philip now has to admit to himself that he does not know what the Unitarians believe. In his ignorance he is simply following the religious dictates of his own family, and he has come to believe that only members of the Church of England can be saved.

The effects of the religious discussion between Weeks and Hayward were particularly strong upon Philip. After he has savored their arguments he finds that he cannot accept the teachings of the Anglican Church any longer. He realizes that these were forced upon him while he was a child and now that he was becoming a man he was able "to put off the faith of his childhood quite simply, like a cloak that he no longer needed." In his new found freedom he found great relief, but, as do many in a similar position, he realizes that most of the rules of religion are still necessary in society on the secular level. He no longer can accept Christianity, but it seems that he must accept Christian ethics, and he marvels at the **irony** in the situation. It is almost as if a man didn't believe in automobiles, yet he must obey the traffic signs.

It is also important to note that without the designs of any particular religion to guide or thwart him Philip actually becomes a better person. He is more concerned with the people about him than ever before, and he makes their humanity his inspiration. But in spite of all of this there comes a thought which does upset Philip's religious revolution. He has come to doubt religion, and he therefore doubts reward and punishment, heaven and hell. If this is true he will never have an afterlife and he will never see his parents, particularly his mother in heaven. It is upsetting, but Philip defends his atheism by the excuse: "I can't help it."

Comment: In the throes of his new found freedom Philip gives himself to experience even more freely than before. He becomes a regular patron of the theatre along with Hayward, and the influence of the modern playwrights stimulates his appetite to participate in life, real life as he refers to it. He is anxious for experience, but not only for sexual experience, for even at this early age he realizes what it has done to those about him. As an example of this he sees Hayward running off for his nightly jaunt into the darkest streets in a quest for satisfaction. But Philip is too much of a realist to accept sex as the only important direction or to distort that drive. Of course the basic inferiority complex has something to do with Philip's withdrawal, but it is also because

he does see that this is only a segment of life - not everything.

Thus Philip is anxious to get back into London to begin the adventure of life. But before he does W. Somerset Maugham steps into the pages with a rather strong editorial on life and ambition. Here the author stresses the illusion of ideals and ambitions and the lies which one age passes on to the next so that it will make the same mistakes. As such he seems to be emphasizing the fact that youth is not essentially a happy time, and that it only becomes golden to those who have lost it. It also offers Mr. Maugham an opportunity to give us something of his literary beliefs at the time. He expresses his feelings in the indictment of Hayward's attitude toward art, which is categorized as idealism. But idealism is not ideal to Maugham as expressed in *Of Human Bondage*, but rather it was a distortion of life with its exaggerated emphasis on emotion and response. It is interesting to note here the basic disagreement which Mr. Maugham has with the value of art and artists in the twentieth century. He seems to be attacking the attitude of the ivory tower and of the artist's elevation above the masses. It is a point of contention too great to decide here, but Mr. Maugham seems to have notable allies in Shakespeare and the early Greek dramatists.

After a year in Germany Philip Carey is anxious to return to England to assume his position in the world as a producer rather than an accepter of life. His experiences in Heidelberg have opened his eyes and mind and heart to the world about him to a degree never known. His final departure is stimulated by Hayward's exit to and letters from Italy, and these prove to be too much of a temptation to resist, so Philip is soon on his own way, but in a different direction - back to England. In a final touch of **irony** Philip realizes as he is about to leave that he has truly been happy in Germany. He has attained the thing which he set out for, and gained a broad scope and knowledge of humanity in the process, and there doesn't seem to be any doubt which Mr. W. Somerset Maugham means to emphasize as more effectual in the life situation. Certainly Philip is not past the age of "growing pains" before maturity, but his German experience has given him a firmer knowledge of himself and of the world because of his exposure to conflicting philosophies and various kinds of people.

In a ironic twist which the author introduces at the end of Philip's year in Germany the boy avoids meeting a friend of his uncle and aunt, a Miss Wilkinson, who is also heading for England and the vicarage at the time. It is ironic because she is to play an important part in the next step on the road to maturity in the life of Philip Carey.

Comment: Germany at this period has symbolic value for Philip and his particular class and generation in England. For Germany symbolized freedom of thought - a land where ethics could be discussed and not simply accepted unthinkingly. Heidelberg, then, is something of a liberation for Philip. He learns more of life and of passion; in the persons of Weeks and Hayward he has the lesson driven home to him that men are not always what they seem on the surface. This is hardly an original observation on Philip's part, but the point is that this is something Philip had to learn. As Plato wrote in The Republic, one of the problems both of the good private citizen,

the private man, and the public man, the judge or legislator, is how he can learn the nature of the evil in men without being guilty of doing evil himself. Philip is learning about man's nature, but he has to learn from experience. Thus, even Weeks cannot really tell him what Hayward is, though Weeks is presented as a strong and scholarly man who knows what he is seeking - wisdom - and who sets about to get it if it can be had. But Philip must learn from experience.

Philip is introduced to philosophy in Heidelberg under several well-known professors, especially Kuno Fischer, and this reinforces Philip's turn of mind which even then, in part because of his childhood sufferings, is somewhat philosophical. But that branch of formal philosophy which is most stressed in *Of Human Bondage* - a branch from which the novel derives its title, from the Ethics of Spinoza - is of course ethics, or the philosophy of man's conduct.

As religion has weakened in its influence on Philip, he finds the need for an alternative, and he seeks it in philosophy of the brand purveyed at Heidelberg. It is perfectly in keeping with the spirit of the work that Philip should listen to lectures on Schopenhauer, a skeptical ethical theorist who posits as the highest good (the summum bonum, as this is technically called in ethics) nothingness or non-being, to put it simply.

Philip, then, returns to England having been exposed to the world and having, after some mistakes of a distinctly minor nature, attained some independence of thought. But the suffering, the "bondage" to irrational passion which is to be the central action of the book, is still ahead of him.

SUMMARY AND CONCLUSION:

These chapters have the following purposes:

1. To place Philip in contact with new ideas and kinds of people, and thereby to illustrate his development.

2. To bring Philip into direct confrontation with a stormy, and somewhat grotesque, affair of passion: that between Herr Sung, the Chinaman, and Fraulein Cacilie.

3. One subsidiary effect of the German experience on Philip is the completion of the undermining of his faith in formal Christianity. At the end of Chapter 27, the American Unitarian theological student, Weeks, gives Philip a copy of Renan's Vie de Jesus. This book, along with Strauss' Leben Jesu, was enormously influential on English and European intellectuals of the later nineteenth century. For the first time, the methods of historical scholarship had been seriously applied to the Bible, and specifically to the Gospels. And the life of Christ is analyzed by what comes to be known as the "higher criticism" of the Bible, of which Renan's work is one of the most famous examples, in such a way that it is stripped of supernatural elements, as an attempt is made to explain them rationalistically. Christ becomes, in this view, not a supernatural figure, much less the Son of God, but simply a man with a lofty ethical teaching.

4. When Philip returns from Germany, then, he has very little in common with his uncle, the Vicar of Blackstable. Spiritually they are now complete strangers, although Philip still has an emotional tie and a genuine affection for his aunt. The German experience has changed and deepened his character, and, it may be, the experience has fortified him for the trials he will now undergo.

FIRST ROMANCE: CHAPTERS 32-35

On his return from Germany Philip Carey was greeted with three situations which were to concern his interests for some time to come. He soon saw a change in his relations with his aunt and uncle; he had to make a decision regarding his profession; and he was greeted by the first strong sexual desire in his life.

His first meeting with his relatives after a year's absence shows that they have aged considerably, but neither has changed appreciably as a person. His uncle the vicar is still a vapid and weak person; his aunt is still living as a support to her husband, and the reader is soon aware that she is worth ten of him. As such Philip has his first insight into their lives as they await death. It is not a bright picture, and Philip is more resolved than ever not to have the same fate.

One of the first questions from the vicar upon Philip's arrival concerns the boy's future and particularly his profession for life. As Philip has no desire to continue his formal education at the great English schools of Oxford and Cambridge, it is suggested that he has only four alternatives of respectability - the Army, the Navy, the Law, and the Church. Again, none of the four stimulate Philip's interest, but since he must make a decision and since he wants to start his life in London he accepts a position as an apprentice to an accountant. Thus, with his profession settled Philip has the summer at his leisure and he is determined to enjoy himself to the fullest.

Philip's first sexual encounter is with Miss Wilkinson, the woman he had taken great pains to avoid on his trip back from Germany. She is about ten years his senior and probably much more, and as such is quite a woman of the world. She, too, had had a religious background as the daughter of a clergyman, but she has rebelled in many ways and lost her convictions. For some years she had been a governess in Germany and most recently in France. She had been very much influenced by her years in France particularly and had picked up an accent and usage of French in conversation which was clearly excessive and artificial. Very soon the reader realizes that she is a poseur, and as such she plays her part rather well, due to Maugham's technical skill in drawing character.

The young man and the older woman are thrown together by circumstances. At first Philip is not particularly happy with the situation, for he feels that he has little in common with her. But Miss Wilkinson has had more experience in the world and she soon intrigues Philip with her **allusions** to the more scandalous sides of Parisian life. She flirts with Philip almost from the start and exaggerates her own references so much that Philip again feels that he is very much of a novice in the affairs of the world. In an attempt not to lose his sense of masculine virility he responds to her promptings by suggestions of his own love affairs in Germany. Soon her influence over him becomes quite strong and Philip, ever impressionable, begins to feel a stronger desire to fulfill himself as a man. As such he is presented as anxious to kiss her and to sweep her off her feet in a schoolboy's distorted concept of the violence of love. He plots to kiss Miss Wilkinson in a secluded section of the garden as they take their nightly stroll together, but indecision causes him to miss his chance. It is a rather frustrating event for Philip (and for Miss Wilkinson as will be shown presently), but it is presented by the author with a combination of tenderness and irony.

The tenderness Mr. Maugham expresses in the situation seems to reflect an awareness of the great emotions which love can generate in the hearts of the lovers. And here our focus is on Philip as he goes through the first confused reactions to his own feelings. But this is not to say that Philip's passion for Miss Wilkinson is love, for even he realizes that it is not. What he feels is the emotional reaction to love itself. As such he makes as much as he can from the situation which leads to the first kiss and beyond.

But W. Somerset Maugham seems also to be pointing out the **irony** of the situation in which Philip finds himself. It is ironic in the sense that Maugham is saying that this is a situation which everyone will know and remember: the first exposure to love and the concomitant sensations of the experience. It is a period of great awkwardness and in this Philip is rather typical of men and women since time began. In their associations they over-emphasize and distort the true sensation of love. A similar situation for a contemporary teenager might find him with the same confused ideas and ideals as Philip as he gropes toward his maturity.

Comment: Thus when Philip does win the kiss and the heart of Miss Wilkinson he also gains something more than what he bargained for. After the quest is over he realizes that the thing sought is not going to be as satisfying as he thought. He is playing the game of love and after a time it becomes boring. The love affair between the young boy and the older woman soon assumes a ridiculous pose. Philip fully realizes as he brings the affair to completion that the situation

is not as important as his passion makes it. Again W. Somerset Maugham seems to be emphasizing that man is driven to the ridiculous by his passions.

Not surprisingly, Philip realizes that his physical conquest of Miss Wilkinson is not satisfactory. His passionate joy is short-lived. He finds that with his passion fulfilled that he can look at the woman with a more objective air, and what he sees in the new light is not attractive. She is probably twice his age. She seems to be finishing life when he is just beginning. It is an awkward situation and Philip is hard-pressed to get out of it.

Quite surprisingly for the present, but quite appropriate for his continuity throughout the book, W. Somerset Maugham now adds a touch of humanity to Miss Wilkinson which the reader has not found before. As Philip tries to break away from the woman the author offers a parallel picture of her becoming so much involved that she is determined not to let him go. It is a device which Mr. Maugham uses throughout his novels, and as such it adds another dimension to the story. Up to this time we have seen the trite ideas which govern her life, the lies which she tells, the poses which she establishes. Now, she is presented as the lonely person, the lost soul who has no home or values to hang on to, and as such it is quite sad. It is certainly sad for Philip, and as such he has much more affection for Miss Wilkinson than when he was driven by passion for her.

Finally, when the summer comes to a close and when Miss Wilkinson must return to Europe, there is the inevitable day of parting. There are the usual tears and the promise of letters which are never to be written. There is the parting at the station, tears and all. It is all very educational for Philip. He has had his first taste of the love affair. In books and in letters (in this situation notably from Hayward, his friend from Germany) and in vulgar stories at school he has heard the distorted fantasy of love. He now realizes how much this differs from reality.

SUMMARY AND CONCLUSION:

These chapters have the following function:

1. Philip becomes further estranged from the vicar, while he continues to be tied (in a good sense) emotionally to his aunt Louisa.

2. Philip settles on a profession. There were only four professions, it was thought, which a gentleman of the period could consider: the Army, the Navy, the Law, and the Church. For Philip, the first two and the last were eliminated automatically by his physical defect and by his unbelief. Philip is presented as at least honest in this; his uncle seems at times to be almost an unbeliever, and yet to be a clergyman of many years standing and practice. Since Philip has not gone to Oxford, by his own choice, he is thought to be precluded from entering the law. He chooses accountancy, really by default, as it is thought to be of professional level; it is not simply "trade," at which persons of Philip's class were brought up to sneer.

3. Finally, Philip loses his innocence to Miss Wilkinson, and the whole experience turns out to be something less than Philip had bargained for. Ultimately, he hopes

that he will be able to cut loose completely and finally from the rather unattractive, pathetic, and aging Miss Wilkinson, and in this he is shown as becoming ruthless, though he is not basically a ruthless man; he has already suffered too much to be so, or at least his suffering has affected him in another way than to make him hard and unkind.

THE WORKING WORLD: CHAPTERS 36-38

Since Philip had agreed to enter the business world in accounting, he was apprenticed to the office of Herbert Carter and Company in London. As ever, Philip is full of doubt and anxiety as he enters into a new stage of his life, and as the author again accents the fears for the boy it points out a concern for the same problem in so many people. The repetition of this idea by W. Somerset Maugham may be interpreted as an example of his sympathy for the plight of the common man, and particularly for the unusual person as he plunges into life.

In the offices of Herbert Carter and Company Philip meets a wide variety of characters. There is Mr. Goodworthy, "an odd mixture of superiority and shyness"; there is Watson, fat, boring, and the son of a beermaker, a product and example of the superior public school pride which Mr. Maugham attacks in many sections of the novel; and there is Mr. Carter himself, a man who wears the title of gentleman without distinction. In this introduction to the working world Philip Carey soon finds the boredom which many million others also suffer. His boredom is also accentuated by his loneliness in London, for he must eat and live alone day after day. His usual shyness prevents him from finding friendship very easily and from accepting invitations from his fellow workers to visit their homes. Philip spends a miserable Christmas alone in the great city, and he gives himself to the depths of self-pity. He finds his own position is such a contrast to that of Watson, and he finds humiliation in his own poverty.

In London Philip is also bombarded by letters from Miss Wilkinson, and the young boy constantly reproaches himself for having entered into a relationship with the older woman. Yet he cannot be so brutal to her as Watson suggests, and his own indecision taunts him. When Watson suggests that he "hook it," that is to ignore completely the pleas of Miss Wilkinson, Philip finds that he both envies Watson and hates him too. He envies his ease in disposing of superfluous women, but he hates his callous nature.

But if Philip is envious of Watson, there is another clerk, Thompson who is envious of Philip. Both of them are in the same type of job in the firm and the other clerk has none of the opportunities that Philip has. Thompson is also more adaptable to business than Philip, and as such Thompson does not waste any chance to criticize Philip for his stupidity. In this situation Philip realizes the enormity of his mistake in selecting the business world for his profession and each day his hatred for the entire life grows. He had expected great things from his life in London and it had only accentuated his misery.

It is after Philip has become desperate that W. Somerset Maugham again rescues him from that situation with a reminder of the artistic talents which Philip has and which offer the young man some solace in his situation. In the boredom of his position in the office Philip turns to drawing and finds that art may offer him a possible release from the oppressive life of London. There is also the solace of a visit from his friend from Germany, Hayward. This wandering Englishman has been to other places on the European continent and has had many experiences while Philip was stuck in the offices of Herbert Carter and Company. But Philip is now a little older and a little wiser and he does not view Hayward with the same feelings as before. Hayward disappoints Philip with his condescending attitude toward life and humanity, and a wiser Philip sees many errors in the philosophy which guides his older friend. It is still another example of Maugham's intention that the reader see the maturing process in his character.

A wonderful example of the external effect of life on young Philip occurs when he is sent to Paris along with Mr. Goodworthy on a business venture. Life in Paris can be a maturing thing for any human being, and as such it is for Philip, but not for the usual reasons. He does not find pleasure in the usual attractions of Paris nightlife, and when he is exposed to it he is quite indifferent. But he does see the way that others react, notably Mr. Goodworthy, who is quite ready to have a "fling" in Parisian society. The author presents this latter character as an example of the contradiction in the lives of many men. While they are in their own towns they are dominated by the rules of society, but away from home they are free to indulge their appetites and interests. In other words, Mr. Maugham seems to be pointing out the hypocrisy which governs so many in their lives. Mr. Goodworthy represents this very obviously as he delights in and then later attacks the looseness of Parisian life.

But Philip's visit to Paris is not taken up completely with Mr. Goodworthy's conduct, for he is greatly attracted to the artistic side of Paris with its great galleries and museums, and the great painters who are represented there. The inspiration of these great artists gives Philip the final impetus to resolve to quit his position with Herbert Carter and Company. And this is exactly what he does when he returns to London. He is quite happy to leave the business world, and it is rather obvious that his employer is not sorry to see him go. But it is a decision which he must explain to his relatives, a second failure via escape from a situation which he was not able to control or adjust to. There is an obvious parallel in Philip's failure in school and in the business world, and it seems to express something of the author's idea of misdirected vocations in this world. Mr. Maugham's presentation may be interpreted as refuting the **clichés** regarding devotion to school and dedication to job. The author implies that happiness and fulfillment in life are often stumbled upon rather than attained.

Chapter 38 of *Of Human Bondage* ends with Philip Carey again on his way back to his uncle and aunt. He has failed again, but he has learned something more of life.

Comment: The world of business, as seen through Maugham's eyes, is represented by the accountant's office of Herbert Carter and Company. This world oppresses Philip's spirit to the point that we rather admire his honesty, and certainly sympathize with him, when he says to Mr. Goodworthy: "I'm afraid it sounds very rude, but I hope from the bottom of my heart that I shall never set eyes on any of you again."

The situation of the "articled clerk" in such an office is perhaps in need of explanation. Philip and Watson have such positions. Instead of being paid a salary from the firm, they had to pay (in Philip's case, three hundred pounds) for the privilege of working in the office as apprentices to the profession. They were offered in exchange for their efforts training and an entrance into the profession. Philip would have had to do this work for five years before he could earn any kind of a real salary, assuming he were successful.

But despite the treatment Philip receives and his hatred of the office, he and Watson are treated as gentlemen learners rather than as hired help. Their positions are contrasted with that of Thompson, who appears in Chapter 38. He is, as he says to Philip bitingly and bitterly: "...not a gentleman. I'm only a clerk. I have a bath on Saturday night." And Thompson, highly resentful of Philip, says to him in this same scene:

> "Will you condescend to do a few sums in simple addition today? I'm afraid it's asking a great deal from a gentleman who knows Latin and Greek."

But Thompson can never advance beyond his present ill-paid clerk-ship, and this rankles in his mind. Maugham here presents what he seems to consider the strait-jacketed class system of the time, and while he basically sympathizes with the idea of the English gentleman, he feels free to satirize the less attractive elements of the system.

Philip, while he loathes Thompson with the rest, has to admit in honesty that the clerk is better at the work than he is. Philip has prospects, even in this profession in which he is not very competent or interested, because he is a gentleman and has been able to put up the sum to pay for his articled apprenticeship. The clerks have a bleak future. They in turn hate Philip, because they see the situation as unjust.

SUMMARY AND CONCLUSION:

These chapters have the following purposes:

1. They present Philip as trying out a profession; like many, if not most young men of his or our own time, he is initially undecided as to what he wants to do or should do in life. He must choose his work, but here, again like many, he makes the wrong choice and regrets it. He knew what he did not want; that was to be ordained and become a minister like his uncle. But here he is presented as having made a choice on a wrong basis, and at least he is honest enough to admit his mistake and get clear. In another sense, then, this has not been a failure for him, but a qualified success, for he has learned much about himself.

2. Here, in his presentation of the "pecking order" of the office, from Mr. Carter down to Thompson, Maugham is satirizing certain of the ideas of class held in England at the turn of the century. But it should be kept in mind that basically he sympathizes with the existing class structure, even while he satirizes it. He sees that class, like the poor, is a concept or entity which in his view will always be with human society.

THE ARTIST IN PARIS: CHAPTERS 39–51

Philip returns to Blackstable and his uncle and aunt with apprehension in his heart. How would they take his resignation from his position in London and his decision to go to Paris to study painting? The vicar regards his resignation as a sign of weakness, for only weak men change their minds. On the other

BRIGHT NOTES STUDY GUIDE

hand Mrs. Carey is genuinely concerned with Philip's next step. It is clear that she loves Philip very much, and that the vicar loves himself. But Philip is determined to get to Paris to study, even if it means that he must sell his late father's jewelry.

The unpleasantness of this situation is finally resolved by Aunt Louisa's generosity. Her life has been taken by giving, particularly giving to her husband, but now her gift is directed toward Philip. Aunt Louisa has saved some money for her old age, but now she insists that Philip have it to further his career in art. It is an example of the genuine love which she bears for the boy, and further represents the fact that she is one of those people who are only completed by going outside of themselves to help others. She is the truly religious person in her household, and she complements her faith with reason and compassion.

It is through Aunt Louisa's generosity that Philip finally realizes just how much she loves him - and how much he loves her. Thus, after the vicar has been appeased, Philip boards the train to leave for Paris and his eyes are filled with tears. In what is one of the memorable scenes of the novel Philip bids goodbye to his aunt until eternity, and the most complete fulfillment of love he has known since the death of his mother touches him. It is a tribute to the talent of W. Somerset Maugham that he brings such emotion to the page. The greatness of the scene is based upon the author's great compassion for mankind.

Philip Carey's arrival in France changes his humor after the tearful parting from his aunt. He is embarking on the greatest adventure of his life, with more freedom that he has ever known. And his spirits cannot be dampened by economic limitations and cold rooms in a fifth floor walk-up. As with many young men in comparable situations he feels that he will be able to withstand any difficulty in dedication to his art, and as such he accepts the ugly side of Parisian life since it is its contrast with the beautiful world which interests him. He finds Paris filled with magic and wants to join in the life of the people and abandon himself to his work.

His feelings here offer an interesting contrast to the life of some other artists who have also come to France from England. An example of this is Mrs. Otter, also an artist, but who will not live as a Parisian in Paris. Her apartment represents her refuge against Paris, for it is a duplicate of thousands found in London. Mr. Maugham seems to use Mrs. Otter as an example of the narrowness of the English attitude which finds that any way which is different is necessarily wrong. But Philip's concerns are not with Mrs. Otter, for he is soon caught up in the artistic world of Amitrano's School. On his first day he meets Fanny Price, an unattractive fellow Englishwoman, and he has his first experience in seeing a nude model pose for his class. He also comes in contact with one of the eccentric geniuses of Paris in the person of Clutton, a man who is meant to represent the dedicated and truly inspired artist. In this situation Philip begins to hear of the new movements in art, the new names which are to become household names for art lovers the world over. And he slowly begins to realize how limited he is himself.

As usual Philip finds that his life soon becomes involved in the lives of the others around him, and as ever it creates emotional problems for him. Philip is always too much of a humanitarian to ignore the problems of his friends, and he has a capacity for cultivating friends with problems. Miss Fanny Price is an example of this, and Philip finds that she is attracted to him romantically while he only has pity on her for the ugly life which she lives. Fanny is dedicated, but ironically she has no talent. She attempts to do with perspiration what she cannot accomplish with inspiration, but of necessity she fails. The point which the author seems to be making here is the frustration of art if there is no talent to support one's interests or desires. W. Somerset Maugham, who knew the life of the struggling artist first-hand, brings out all of the misery and deprivation which must accompany the artist's dedication. He implies that it is worthwhile in the life of a great painter or musician, but what of the second-rate artist, is it worth his life and death? It is a question which Philip Carey will have to face before long.

Two other people are offered to the reader as a part of the whole which constitutes the artistic world of Paris. The first is Flanagan, and the second is Lawson. Both are Americans and they are contrasts in virtually everything but their interest in art. And even here there are basic differences in values. Neither is particularly talented, although Lawson is better than Flanagan, and it is fortunate for him that he is. The point here is that Flanagan is much less dedicated than Lawson, and defeat does not mean as much to him as it would to Lawson. But for the moment the thing which all three friends think least of it defeat - the world has to accept their talents!

It is through his new friends that Philip meets and comes under the influence of an eccentric poet-philosopher, Cronshaw, who is to be an important force in Philip's later life. It is now that Cronshaw influences Philip's attitude toward art, but in later years he is going to influence the young man's philosophy of life. Cronshaw does not accept the point that art is the only, or most important, consideration in life. Cronshaw insists that art is a luxury for the rich and that they collect the work of the poor. He has lived a life dedicated to pleasing himself without concern for the principles of art or of society. In some way it is suggested that he has attained satisfaction in his belief, but Philip is to know otherwise before he lays the body of Cronshaw to rest some years later.

In the development of Philip's life in London it turns out that Cronshaw and Fanny Price are the two most important forces acting upon him. It is not that he accepts the philosophy or society of each one completely, but from each he receives something which is going to direct the course of his future life. Philip's association with Fanny is always difficult. As noted above she was the first one to aid him at Amitrano's school, but before long Philip is able to recognize (as does everyone else but Fanny) that her work is not good and that she has no future at all in art. In one of the most memorable scenes in the entire book Fanny's work is completely devastated by an important critic, whose advice to "try dressmaking" is the final insult to her. But Fanny is oblivious to criticism and will not take the critic's word. Instead she turns on her friends and severely criticizes Philip. It is her means of covering her own shame and sorrow, and she soon returns to ask Philip's forgiveness. It is at this time that Philip realizes how much she loves him, and it is a situation which he cannot accept. He does escape from her for the summer, and when the fall comes he is relieved that she is no longer at school or in the usual haunts of the artists.

Thus Philip goes on to other interests, and in their variety both the character and the readers forget about Fanny for the present. But both are awakened quite forcefully when Philip is given a suicide note from Fanny some months later. As ever Philip is concerned about his friends and he rushes to save her. But Fanny is past saving - she has hanged herself. Of course Philip feels somewhat guilty for her death, and he accuses himself. But obviously he has had little to do with her demise, for W. Somerset Maugham has other culprits to accuse. It is certainly society which is guilty, but more particularly it is art. It is the artistic temperament which so drives talented people to sacrifice themselves. It is a very poignant indictment of the overall values of art in this world and of those who would distort its

value and purpose. To these Maugham subtly offers the example
of Fanny Price. The question is certain to arise whether art
is not worth the sacrifice of a thousand Fanny Price's for the
attainment of one great picture or poem or symphony, and the
author seems to emphasize that there are human and humane
considerations which supersede the call of art.

Fanny is put to rest by Philip and her brother. The latter is
shown to be a miserly person who would not help his sister
when she was in dire need, but who is now content to spend a
good deal more while he is in Paris in a tour of the nightclubs.
The **irony** in the situation is repulsive to Philip. And when he
bids goodbye to Fanny's brother it is not the last time her face
will cross his memory.

Cronshaw, the poet, sheds some light on the world at this
point in Philip's life. He is the typical example of the Parisian
artist who has given all to stay in a life which is meant for him.
Nor does he pretend or contend that this is making him happy.
He is living in poverty and perversity, and has no concern for
what posterity will think of his work. His philosophy is similar to
predestination, and he challenges all of man's actions with this
point. His points are very illuminating to Philip, but this is not
to say that the younger man agrees with or follows the teaching
of the other. Cronshaw shows Philip that since he is following
the ethics based on Christianity, Philip is accepting the religion
which he insists on denying. On the other hand Cronshaw says
that goodness and evil have no meaning for him on a religious
or social level, and thus he becomes independent of them. As he
says: "I am the measure of all things. I am the center of the world."

In the midst of Philip's emotional and educational
involvement in art, W. Somerset Maugham changes the pace
somewhat by reintroducing Hayward, Philip's friend from

Germany. Hayward is still as vacuous as ever, and as ever he is subtly suggesting that he has the seed of great work in him and that it will be coming to harvest soon. But by this time Philip is much too mature to bow slavishly to Hayward's erudition. In fact he wants to show off his own learning. Hayward is a novice in art, but he still tries to bluff his way. And this gives Philip the opportunity to cut him down to size. In short order Hayward's opinions are deflated and Philip's superior knowledge wins out. Of course it is humorous that Philip's knowledge is not his own, merely a parroting of what he has been told by his own friends. But Philip does shine in the situation, and he compensates somewhat for his own stupidity in philosophy when he was with Hayward previously.

Philip is also introduced to the passions of Parisian life in the affair between his fellow artists Ruth Chalice and Lawson. While he is away on a summer holiday with them he sees them become lovers, and this instills a greater need for love in his life. But it was not the type of love which his friends were experiencing. Philip needed a more elevated love, something which would smack of the mystical as well as the physical. He could very easily imagine that he was Ruch Chalice's lover when he was away from her, but when she was present the desire faded. As the author notes in Chapter 42 Philip was in love with love, and here Mr. Maugham points out the distinction between the real and ideal in love. Philip had already experienced some of this dissatisfaction in his affair with Miss Wilkinson, and he had too much intelligence to fall into the trap again at this time. His intellect aids him now, but it is to falter at another and far more important time.

The section on Philip's life in Paris would provide a liberal education in art for most readers of the novel, for W. Somerset Maugham has included comment and discussion on some of the leading artists of the last century. Some of this may go too far in its discussion, for the average reader is not aware of the many names and certainly not aware of the stylistic differences in the artists mentioned. It is with this in mind that an appendix of authors has been included at the end of this work.

As Philip remains in Paris, and particularly after the death of Fanny Price, he becomes more concerned with his own value as an artist. When he set out for Paris he was content to learn the art slowly, and he realized that there was so much that he had to learn. But now that he had been in Paris and seen the life and the artistic and emotional problems associated with it, he began to wonder if this was not another mistake in a series of mistakes which had plagued his life. Art was important to him, but he began to question the values which it contained. He has seen immensely talented as well as untalented people by this time, and all were sure that they had the gift and that fame and fortune would come if they just persevered. Even Clutton, who obviously had a greater talent than the rest of those whom Philip knew, was living a life which was full of struggles. Even Philip's own teachers had not received the success or reward which they desired.

In a final effort to see if his work is worth the years of sacrifice, and also to see if he has progressed any beyond his original ability, Philip decides first upon entering his work in the annual student competition. He is rejected by the committee and dejected because the works of his friends have been accepted. Even Flanagan, the American who only works half-heartedly, has his picture accepted. Then Philip boldly confronts his teacher, Foinet, and much to the student's surprise the teacher accepts the invitation to see Philip's work and to evaluate his total effort. In what turns out to be another momentous decision in Philip Carey's life, the Frenchman tells him that his talent is not worth all the struggle and the sacrifice of normal relationship which art requires.

It is with mixed feelings that Philip receives the news, for on a negative side it represents still another failure in his life. He has not found success in the art world as he did not find it in the business world, or in the educational world. It must be a great disappointment to try so diligently and to fail. But on the other hand there is something positive in Philip's defeat, for he has learned what not to do, and that is certainly a step in the right direction. At this point the author also introduces an interesting sidelight into the humanity of the teacher, Foinet, for in his decision to tell Philip to abandon his work as an artist there is more than a suggestion that the teacher wishes that he had given the same advice to himself a half century before. And of course this is related to the over-all message which F. Somerset Maugham seems to be directing to the reader: in effect he says that there are many more important things in this world than art, and that man cannot distort his life to allow art to dominate all of his existence. Foinet tells Philip to give up because he is only mediocre, but there is the point that the teacher is in the same category.

But before Philip is able to leave there are to be some important words with the poet Cronshaw. In his first few months in Paris Philip had been quite taken with Cronshaw as a romantic symbol of a man's complete devotion to being himself, come hell or high water. But Philip was too practical to accept all the philosophy of the poet. Cronshaw had produced a volume of poetry to show for all of his life, and at this time there was little that he felt for it even. He had no designs for publication of his work, and seemed to disdain everything which the commercial world represented. But when Philip approaches the poet with the question of sacrificing his young life to the demands of the old art, Cronshaw finally allows a moment of clear perspective to enter into his thoughts. When Philip tells him of his idea of "chucking" art, the poet replies, "Why shouldn't you?" Philip answers "I suppose I like the life," and in the moment of revelation Cronshaw utters in disbelief "This?" And then after a pause he continues "If you can get out of it, do while there is time."

The recognition that Cronshaw has wasted his life comes to both the poet and the painter at the same time. It is a moment of truth for them both. And one cannot help feeling pity for the wasted Cronshaw, who once had the same youthful vitality as Philip. Thus, with Foinet's advice in his ears and Cronshaw's warning in his heart, Philip prepares to leave Paris, but there is one more setback which is to come. A letter from his uncle informs him that Aunt Louisa is dead. Thus when Philip Carey moves once more across the English Channel it represents the close of two eras in his life. The person who made his study of painting possible is dead, and the **irony** is that in a sense his desire to be an artist is dead, too. Leaving Paris Philip is more alone than ever. The combination of death and failure might turn any one to despair. Yet, Philip is quite able to bounce back after his defeat - and years later he is to realize how defeat is necessary for victory.

Comment: The life of art is shown to have value in these chapters, provided that the individual who leads it

a. Has unusual talent.

b. Is prepared to give up everything for it, so that in order to actualize his talent he will forsake the world almost in a religious sense.

Philip's experience here may be compared profitably with that of Strickland, mentioned earlier as the hero of The Moon and Six-pence, who in turn was based on an actual artist, Paul Gauguin, who had been in business in France when at the age of forty he abandoned his family, and went to Tahiti to develop into a great painter and ultimately to die horribly of leprosy. Yet his life - even as personified in the cruel and ruthless character of Charles Strickland - has meaning for Maugham.

Philip, on the other hand, finds from his teacher that he has technical competence, yes, but no unusual talent. He will fail as an artist, as do over 99% of those who would embrace this calling. But Philip has the honesty and the flexibility to see these limitations, and to return again to England and to the vicar. The occasion of his return is the death of his Aunt Louisa, but he would have returned anyway and admitted his mistake; we are sure of this from our analysis of his character so far. His return, then, is an outward failure, just as has been his abandonment of the accounting profession. But it is a victory, a victory over himself. This is in part established by a contrast with what happens to Miss Fanny Price. Unable to stand the thought that she has permanent limitations - that she is, in other words, finite in capability - she hangs herself in a despairing gesture of defiance against the wretchedness of life. Her suicide has a deep effect on Philip. But her reaction was an excessive deed; she could have freed herself from human bondage, but she chose not to. Suicide, it is implied here, is a cowardly way to resolve life's problems. Later Philip is to sink to similar depths of

poverty and misery, but perhaps the memory of Miss Price saves him from a similar act.

SUMMARY AND CONCLUSION:

These chapters have the following functions:

1. An introduction for Philip into the life of real poverty and squalor. The harrowing scenes which will come later and which involve Philip personally are in part thus made more believable.

2. An examination of art and the life of art as a substitute for religion in terms of its ability to sustain man spiritually. The final conclusion is skeptical: art is worthwhile only if the artist has decided talent and probably genius, and is prepared to give up everything in the furtherance of his art. Otherwise, it ranges from a cheap pose (as in Hayward), to a pitiful ending (as in Fanny Price).

3. Some introduction to aesthetics and the philosophy of art, in which Maugham has long been interested, for in common with James Joyce, Maugham seeks in art one of the possible alternatives to revealed religion which will sustain man in an age which has come to doubt religion. Art almost becomes a secular religion, though bringing tragedy rather than spiritual sustenance to many, in Maugham's view. It is not the only such panacea or possible substitute in this novel; the idea of progress - social betterment - is another, and is also largely discounted by Maugham, as we shall see.

A NEW DIRECTION: CHAPTERS 52-53

When Philip returns to Blackstable for his aunt's funeral, he finds that life in the vicarage is very much the same. At least the vicar is very much the same. He is rather unmoved by his wife's death, an aspect which might be based on the rather celebrated British reserve, but in this case it seems to Philip that the uncle really doesn't feel badly about the passing of his wife. Oh, he will miss her cooking, and their occasional game of cards which he had to win, but otherwise life will go on very much the same with Louisa dead. In this situation Philip realizes more than ever how much of a fraud and hypocrite his uncle is.

An example of the uncle's hypocrisy is his concern for the number of wreaths which will come to honor his wife. It becomes quite a contest to outdo the last funeral in the area. And, fortunately for the vicar, there are more wreaths this time. Nor is the uncle the only hypocrite, for the townspeople are as little concerned as the husband, but they put up a pretense of sorrow by closing their shops for the day - or at least for half of it. To Philip it is all so shoddy. Aunt Louisa deserved more than this. After the funeral Philip has enough time to think of what he would do next. Away from Paris he is able to view it more objectively, and he is more convinced that he has made the right step in leaving the world of art. But this brings up the next point: what can he turn to now? Oddly enough it is the vicar who prods him to a decision.

Of course the vicar is quite available to criticize Philip's return - and he is almost as critical as when the boy left. The vicar views a decision as a decision - it cannot be changed, and, if it is, it shows a lack of intellect or decency. At least it is wrong.

Thus when he taunts Philip about his next step in life the boy responds almost automatically that he is going into medicine. "He resolved then and there to enter his father's old hospital in the autumn." This quote from the book seems to emphasize the boy's spur-of-the-moment decision, but the author may be reflecting upon the give and take in life which so often decides a job or a vacation. Certainly, the idea of studying medicine was not new to Philip, but it was surprising for him to realize how appropriate it would be. Of course his uncle has to offer some remark, and when he questions Philip on what the boy learned in Paris Philip is more sure than ever that it was a worthwhile venture. The uncle accuses Philip of being flippant, and Philip realizes that it is true.

Flippancy is necessary because it saves Philip from taking the values of the world too seriously. He had searched through the works of the great philosophers and come to his own personal rule: "Follow your inclinations with due regard to the policeman around the corner." This was based on the concept that there was no such thing as good or evil, and it shows the influence of Darwin's Origin of Species. Philip felt a new freedom. There are no limitations to his actions - only the rules which society adopts. But, in spite of this, Philip was not about to give himself to the excess of passion. He was always too intelligent to do that.

In the throes of his speculation he is reminded of Cronshaw's riddle of the Persian carpet, and the message is a concern to him. As Cronshaw said, there was no answer to the riddle unless you found it out yourself. Little did Philip realize that he was unraveling the threads of the riddle as he prepared to make his third start in life in the medical profession.

Comment: In this section, Philip is seen as he formulates a working philosophy based on Hobbesian principles that the only thing which restrains man is naked force: "the policemen round the corner." Thus, the latter half of Chapter 53 should be read with particular care, although there is a maximum of speculation and a minimum of action here. The philosophers whom Philip reads and admires are Thomas Hobbes, Spinoza, and Hume - but Spinoza above all.

Philip seems to become a relativist in ethics. This means that as far as the individual is concerned, there are no absolute moral standards. There is no sin; however, there is positive law, as represented by the policeman round the corner, and if the individual breaks the law, he must and will be punished, or else there would be no public order, and life would be, in the words of Hobbes, "nasty, brutish, and short." Philip is still engaged in explaining to his own satisfaction the figure in the carpet; the figure of the Persian Carpet which his friend and mentor Cronshaw has presented to him as a solution to the riddle of life.

As we see Philip at the end of this section, he is starting out to London with his sixteen hundred-pound fortune - actually, a considerable sum of money though by no means wealth - to study medicine. The suddenness of his decision to become a doctor of medicine is intended to illustrate the casualness with which men make, more often than not, binding lifetime decisions.

SUMMARY AND CONCLUSION:

These chapters have the following purposes:

1. They provide some further insight into the bases of Philip's new ethical theory which he has formulated for himself with the aid both of formal philosophical writing and of experience.

2. They show Philip once again turning to a new profession, rather casually, because with two previous apparent failures he is not likely to embrace a third profession enthusiastically.

A THIRD BEGINNING: CHAPTERS 54-55

Philip left Blackstable and his uncle to begin his third venture into the world when he was generally older than the other medical students with whom he would be studying. But this did not bother him. The two or three years which the uncle might view as wasted were a good background for his new life. Philip chose St. Luke's hospital because it had been the place of his father's training.

On the day of his arrival Philip has his first class in anatomy and he has his first look at a human leg which he and another student are to share in dissecting. He meets his new fellow students, Dunsford and Newsome, and gets to know quite a bit about the background of all of the new men. W. Somerset Maugham, who knew the inside of a hospital from the same vantage point as Philip, seems to delight in giving the reader some insight into the lives of the men who compose the medical fraternity. The author emphasizes that they are of various dispositions and talents, and that in every entering class there are loafers, drifters, and dumb men, as well as diligent, dedicated, and brilliant men. Some of the men are older than Philip, and they seem to be taking up medicine as a last resort, after having failed elsewhere.

One of the most impressive of the upperclassmen whom Philip notices is Griffiths, a rather humorous and well-liked person who is sure to be a success as a doctor. Philip envies Griffiths' ease and amiability, and he pictures himself in the other man's shoes.

Soon after his arrival at the college the routine of everyday work sets in, and Philip finds that he is still not able to fit into the usual activities because of his bad foot and because of the limitations it puts upon his activities and his personality. Soon he enters into the same type of shell which surrounded his earlier life at King's School, but there is a difference this time - for now he is more on his own, and he can count less on someone helping him to escape from any unpleasant situations. It is all a part of maturity, and the author may be implying that the loneliness of Philip is in reality the loneliness of all mankind.

Philip does find some aid in the friendship of Dunsford, who is not as bright or talented as Philip, but who does have a happy disposition and outlook on life. Dunsford is not complex at all, and W. Somerset Maugham may be playing with the word "dunce" in his name and ability. But if Dunsford is important for anything in the novel, he is most notable for his introduction of Philip to the waitress Mildred, the novel's embodiment of man's "bondage" to passion.

Comment: Entrance into a medical school was much less difficult for a man of Philip's classical education

than it probably would be today. However, the examinations assured at least a moderate amount of knowledge before the candidate could be graduated and practice medicine. They demanded some study and concentration. Medical students did not take courses - they listened to lectures and did practical work.

Philip's classmates are exclusively male; women were generally not considered suited for the study and practice of medicine in England and America at the time.

The dwelling on the physical - the body and the ills to which it is subject, may seem morbid, but it is a necessary part of Philip's education. Ultimately, it deepens his understanding of life, and increases his desire to find some way of life which will satisfy him and make the fullest use of whatever ability he has.

The dangers of the medical career are emphasized by the reference at the end of Chapter 54 to the student who died of a pin-prick or cut acquired while dissecting. He died of septicaemia, or blood-poisoning; exactly what Philip's father had died of.

While English medicine was good for the time, it should be remembered that medicine was, by our standards, still in its infancy, and in the absence of the knowledge we have, and with the total lack of antibiotic drugs and advanced techniques of surgery, medicine must have been a grim trade indeed for the average practitioner.

SUMMARY AND CONCLUSION:

In these chapters, Philip turns once again to a new career, and it appears that his father's profession, with its combination of the technical and the humanitarian and humanistic, is likely to suit him at last. But this is the period of calm before the storm.

OBSESSION: CHAPTERS 56–63

The entire sequence with Mildred Rogers is the most perplexing part of this great novel. W. Somerset Maugham points out how reluctantly Philip Carey allows her to grow upon him, but there is nothing to stop the growth. Philip realizes that she is a very shallow person, that she is selfish, that she is not very intelligent nor very attractive - but this is based on reason, and love, or passion, has very little to do with reason. Soon Philip realizes that he must see her every day, and when she is indifferent or mean to him it only stimulates his appetite further. He is obsessed with her, so much so that nothing else seems to matter. He comes to know much of the feeling of despair which must have filled Fanny Price's soul when she was in love with him - but this is no consolation to one who is in the throes of desire.

The entire opening sequence of Philip's relationship with Mildred Rogers shows W. Somerset Maugham's great ability to understand and to project the depths of human character. The author seems to be making the point that love can come in any degree and to anyone, without validity or consistency. Philip is quite a brilliant person, yet he finds that he is obsessed with a woman who is obviously his inferior in wit and personality, in social state and decency. When he is away from her he can reason that she is not worth his concern, that his love is wasted on a shallow and mean girl. But when he is near her all his reason fades as he feels the magic of love invade his soul and the passion of love stimulate his body.

But as interested as Philip is in Mildred, she has no interest in him. All of his efforts meet with failure as he tries to win her friendship and her love. She is indifferent to whatever he does, and Philip is nearly distracted by her actions. He thinks that if he could only have the satisfaction of cutting her down as curtly as she does him it would be enough to drive this madness from his heart, but she never gives him the opportunity. It is only because of his ability to draw that she is finally attracted to him, and with this opening Philip is able to persuade her to come to dinner and the theater with him.

But Philip is not the only person who is romantically attracted to Mildred Rogers. There is competition for the waitress from a German alien, and Philip places a poor second to his efforts at this time. When Mildred does agree to a date with Philip it is only because the German is out of town. And on the date Philip is soon aware of how much more shallow and self-centered she is than he originally believed. She is only impressed by a display of wealth and position, and Philip is forced to spend a good deal of his dwindling funds on her. But he does it gladly - he must have Mildred if he has to buy her and if it costs him his entire fortune.

Mildred Rogers is the girl he loves, and it is incredible to Philip. All the ideals and dreams which Philip had for the woman he would marry are contradicted by this waitress. She is not beautiful. Her skin is yellow-tinged. She is flat-chested. She does not read good literature; knows nothing of art and music; has very few social graces. It is incredible that he could be in love with her - but he is and he would sell his soul for her. As such Philip seems to characterize what W. Somerset Maugham has been saying in a number of sequences in this novel: that love and anguish are interwoven, especially in youth, and that the pangs of love are evils which all humanity must suffer on the way to maturity.

Naturally Philip is not satisfied with the situation. His heart cries out for Mildred and she does not care for him at all. He is merely a ticket to a movie or a dinner in a fashionable restaurant - and all the time her interest is directed to the German. Yet Mildred is not all bad. At the most unexpected times the author will allow her a bit of humanity and feeling which are quite attractive for the moment, although it is somewhat inexplicable and irritating to Philip when she returns to her old ways. What is probably the point here is that the author was not at liberty to make Mildred so intensely evil that the reader would refuse to consider her as a true character at all. But in the overall design she comes close to being the very picture of evil and selfishness. It is seldom that the reader can have any affection for Mildred. Even when she is undergoing great poverty and suffering the general reaction will be that she deserves it. As such the reader can dismiss Mildred rather easily, but not Philip Carey. He is obsessed with her.

Among the points of shallowness in the make-up of Mildred Rogers are her indifference, her lies, and her pride. To Philip she seems quite frigid, and eventually when he wins her kisses they are given with all the enthusiasm of a maiden aunt for a crying child. She constantly tries to hide the fact of her own poverty, and she invents the most outlandish lies. And, ironically, she is quite proud, as evidenced by her behavior to waiters and to the general public. In this same vein, she never says that she would like to go out with Philip or that she would enjoy this play or that show. She merely says "I don't mind," and it is this condescending attitude which annoys Philip to the point of despair.

The course of love for Philip is rough, indeed. Virtually every time that they are put together there is a fight or scene, and it is always Philip who is most miserable from it. In fact Mildred is eternally indifferent. Thus Philip has to beg and promise and buy expensive presents before he is forgiven. And then it starts all over again. On one occasion Mildred lies to him and breaks a date to go out with Miller, her German friend. Philip doesn't accept her excuse and catches her in the lie as she waits for Miller outside her shop. This leads to a bitter scene and Mildred angrily denounces Philip for spying on her. The result finds Philip in his most bitter mood and he exhibits a bit of his manliness and determines that he will have nothing to do with her again. Ironically, the next day he is again begging at her door for just one more chance.

In the chaos of this situation it is not surprising that Philip falters in his studies and that he is on the road to dismissal from the hospital. He fails his major examination, and must sit back and accept the condolences of men who have not half his ability. He realizes more fully what others have suffered from him now that he is the one who is afflicted. And in this respect it is interesting to speculate whether it is Maugham's intention to show that man's evil actions and his lack of concern for others will not be returned in kind and degree some day. Certainly Philip was never as brutal and indifferent to Fanny Price as Mildred is to him, but there is a similarity.

After his dismal showing in the examination Philip is despondent. He is so angry with himself that he feels he must suffer even more, and in this mood of despair he turns to the only person in the world whom he cares for. It is Mildred, and he realizes how futile it would be to expect any consolation from her. Yet, in a turn of events which is most unexpected he receives a warm welcome from her at her shop. It is a sudden twist such as this which keeps the novel from degenerating into a documentary of the social worker, and it shows W. Somerset Maugham's mastery of form and suspense. He is well aware that life has its moments of great turmoil, but it also has its bright side. It is certainly the bright side which Philip Carey sees as he returns to find that Mildred is not angry. She is as bold and as impassive as ever, and Philip finds that he would like to kiss and to stab her at the same time, but he is so much taken by her that he is willing to humble himself to any degree if only he can have her back again.

So Philip again begins his chase, and again the money disappears on expensive dinners and presents. Mildred is impressed, and she refers to him now as she was to refer to him so many times again as "a gentleman in every sense of the word." Philip's gentility, however, does not diminish his desire for her any, and her indifference to him in regard to romance merely whets his appetite more than ever. It is usual that man wants the thing in this world which is slightly beyond him. It is always clear that Mildred does not care for Philip in anything resembling a romantic way, and she is either attracted to him for his money or for the convenience which he offers. Whenever they fight she will remind him that he must take her as he finds her. And Philip does just that.

Philip becomes so obsessed by Mildred that he sacrifices his integrity and principles for her, finally lowering himself so that he uses his club-foot as a source of pity. Surprisingly enough Mildred does react to this plea, and it is one of the most touching moments in the entire novel, for it shows a side of her character which the reader is surprised to find. Since it is so unexpected it is quite impressive. Here, again, the author seems to be balancing Mildred's character, as though he were insuring the reader that a person could not be as completely evil as she seems to be. When she is reduced to tears after hearing Philip's complaint of the world's bitterness to him because of his deformity, it seems that she will be a better person. But such is not the author's design.

Soon Philip and Mildred are again battling, and Philip finds himself so confused that he wishes for the end of love while he hopes that it will never end. He yearns for the peace of soul which he had before she invaded his life, and he still wants to have and possess Mildred more than anything in the world. The world of art and painting and literature become unimportant, for Philip's mind is filled with passion - clouded by lust for Mildred. He must have her as his mistress, if only for a weekend. Then he might be able to erase her from his mind and soul. But he must have her first. In this relation it is interesting to speculate about the author's intentions, for he seems to be developing the idea of Philip's passion to such a state that he is temporarily a changed man. The author may be reminding us that man is not merely an animal, and that when he acts as an animal he is violating his own nature. Certainly Philip's animality dominates his rationality here, and the consequences of this raging desire, quite uninformed by spiritual values, are driving him to despair. On a lower level the author may be reminding us that man must go through these trials in order to master himself. "He that ruleth his own spirit is greater than he that taketh a city," as the proverb attributed to Confucius states the case.

Philip schemes to take Mildred to Paris for a holiday and to make her his mistress. He has some success, for the idea of Paris is delightful, but she offers some slight resistance since it would not be proper to travel with him alone. And by this time Philip is ready to do anything to win her, even to propose marriage. At first the thought of marriage is cast aside, but eventually Philip is ready to wed Mildred if only he can have her. It is a decision which violates every intellectual fiber in his mind, but it is one which will offer ease to his tortured body. As he contemplates his proposal of marriage Philip realizes that disaster is coming, but he is powerless to stop.

But when Philip does propose he is rejected. Mildred is not even subtle about her rejection, for Philip does not have enough money to satisfy her. Since he is a student and living on a budget until he becomes a doctor she feels that it would not improve her own position to marry him (by this time she has not abandoned her pretentions of wealth entirely). Her refusal is a wonderful thing for Philip, as he realizes later in his life, but for the present it is a terrible blow to his pride. He felt sure that his offer would be accepted, if only for the reason of money. Thus he becomes quite angry with her, and allows himself some of the expressions of disgust which he had stored in his heart for so long. The reader is bound to encourage him in his break from Mildred, but Philip is again restrained by the depth of his passion, and the hope that he may still satisfy it.

The results of Philip's emotional strain carry over to his next major examinations at the hospital, when he fails his test in anatomy. But as mortified as he is, Philip cannot escape from Mildred. He makes an heroic effort to seduce her, plotting and encouraging her to come to Paris with him. And he feels that she is really convinced to come when she again confounds him by treating him with affection on their next meeting. She asks him to take her to dinner, and Philip's heart leaps. But then Philip is crushed: Mildred announces that she is going to be married to

Miller. Philip is so overcome with grief that he cannot think, but his instinct carries him through a sad parting as he wishes her good luck and says good-bye.

The first sequence of Philip's obsession with Mildred Rogers is over. She is gone but not forgotten. She has given him an education in emotion. But he still has so much more to learn.

Comment: In these chapters, we learn what the title really means. By human bondage, both Maugham and Spinoza refer to irrational passion: to man sinking beneath his proper nature to be governed by the worst part of his psyche. Philip realized that he is destroying himself; he will spend his small amount of money, which is the only thing that can keep him going until he qualifies as a doctor; in fact, he will jeopardize his professional future. Still, he seems caught in the grip of forces too strong for him to control. This is more than physical passion, actually; it is, as has been said before, an obsession, which is by definition irrational.

These chapters are the heart of the book: the source and the illustration of what the title means. They are by no means fantastic, for the popular newspapers every day have stories that are equally as strange. But Maugham excels in showing a man in torment, despite what his reason tells him. Philip could break off with Mildred, but he does not dare - his affections are trampled upon, but still he asks for more punishment. Maugham is an artist, not a reporter, in his presentation of Philip's situation, and he convinces us that the portrait is a true one.

SUMMARY AND CONCLUSION:

These chapters, then, illustrates the meaning of the title of the novel, for Philip is in truth in the worst form of bondage, and what is even worse, knows it and also knows that he is powerless.

AN EMOTIONAL OASIS: CHAPTERS 64 AND 65

Philip Carey tries to be practical about the departure of Mildred Rogers. His brain dictates his actions, but his heart is not in agreement. Yet, even in the sadness of his life Philip shows the quality of which he is made when he purchases an expensive wedding gift for the couple. He can't afford it, and there is no necessity to do it, but his intentions are good. They are good but they are not perfect, however, as indicated by the showy gift which he selects. Its gaudiness reflects Mildred's taste and is an example of how shallow and unsubstantial she is.

Fortunately Philip's loss is compensated for somewhat by the arrival of his friend Hayward, and it is through an association with him that Philip is able to release some of his sorrow. He again turns to the arts for some consolation, and he has the cooperation of the seasons to aid him. It is spring and nature is in bloom, and certainly art and spring will revive him - or so he hopes.

As usually occurs when he is with Hayward, Philip is soon caught up in the philosophy of life. They are both intelligent people and their discussions generally run to ideals and more broad questions than the daily newspaper. Typical of this is the situation which develops when Hayward asks Philip if he likes the medical profession. Philip assures his friend that he is becoming a doctor only because there is nothing else to do. In their discussions the **theme** is often the vacuity of the average person's life. Thus it again seems proper to reflect upon their conversation as a possible reflection of the philosophy of W. Somerset Maugham himself. The **theme** seems to be that man is directed by powers beyond his control, that man does not do what he wants, but what he is forced to do. Of course this is not the first time that the two friends take up this point, but it is the first time that Philip can add anything of importance based on his own experiences. And again the discussions show how much W. Somerset Maugham is interested in the people who populate his novels - and the people who read them.

It is also at this time that Philip first mentions his desire to travel when he finishes his medical study. He has the itch for foreign and exotic places, and this again represents his attitude of the dreamer and the escapist. He has been a dreamer and escapist ever since his days in school when he wanted to wish away the clubfoot and the class bully. He has wished himself into and out of almost every situation in his life, and generally he is not sorry for his attitude. Nor is he sorry for his failures, especially for the failure in Paris, for it has given him an awareness of beauty which is cheap at any cost.

Comment: The showy dressing-bag, which Philip buys as a wedding present for Mildred at a cost of twenty pounds - a sum of money which might have later, in his days of dire poverty, represented enough to keep him for months - symbolizes both Mildred's tawdry self and Philip's alloyed self-abnegation. Philip delights in abasing himself at this point, but through the gift he is psychologically striking back at Mildred and showing her what she is. "You were bound to accept the highest bidder," he says to her.

In Chapter 64, Philip refers in a talk with Hayward, almost on the day on which Mildred is to be married to Miller, to Keats' Ode on a Grecian Urn. This famous poem deals with permanence - the eternality of art - in the midst of life and its transitoriness. "Thou shalt remain, in midst of other woe than ours, a friend to man - To whom thou say'st / Beauty is truth, truth beauty..." The symbol of the urn is an apt one here, and it is tied up with the ending of *Of Human Bondage*, for Philip is to quote this poem again, upon his marriage: "Forever wilt thou love and she be fair." But this is many years in the future. Meanwhile Philip suffers, although he knows himself that it is in an unworthy and even despicable cause.

SUMMARY AND CONCLUSION:

The purpose of these chapters is to form an emotional interlude or oasis between the hopeless scenes of passion on the part of Philip which have come earlier, and the coming degradation which he is to undergo as a result of this storm of passion. For the time approaches when Philip is to be truly in bondage, from which he barely escapes with his life.

PEACE: CHAPTERS 66-68

The memory of Mildred Rogers still fills Philip's mind for many days after she departs. Now, however, that memory is taking on different associations. The memory of his actions and how he cringed before so coarse a person plague his life. In the cool light of his life he is ashamed of his actions, and he refers to his relationship to Mildred humorously as "six months hard labor."

Philip's activities at school and his associations with his friends tend to take his mind away from Mildred. One of his qualities is that he is able to bounce back from despair, and at this time he bounces first back into his association with his friend Lawson, the painter. And through Lawson Philip receives the Persian rug which the poet Cronshaw said contained the answer to life's riddles. Cronshaw had sent it to Philip, and when he received it Philip was again intrigued by the symbolism which Cronshaw had placed in it. It was a riddle which Philip was to ponder for many years before he discovered its simple answer.

Another person whom Philip meets through his friends is Mrs. Norah Nesbit. At first, after his recent frustration with Mildred, Philip is not particularly interested in developing his relationship with Norah. Yet, within a week he has found that she is so pleasant that he is attracted to her strongly and finds peace and contentment in her company. Norah represents quite a contrasts to Mildred in almost every detail. And every point of contrast is an asset for Norah. Mildred was selfish, mean, and moody. Norah is helpful, happy, and delightful. She is quite similar to Philip is her interests and she obviously has a finer brain and sense of culture than Mildred. Therefore, it is rather easy for Philip to start a romance with Norah. It is not the same feeling that he had for Mildred. It is more like admiration than love, and it gives an ease in his relationship with Norah which was never present with Mildred.

As a result of the peace found in Norah's company Philip is able to concentrate on his studies and he passes his examinations with ease. Norah is encouraging, not demanding, and he thrives physically and spiritually under her care. She is such a simple person that she begins to attract Philip's views. She, too, is engaged in artistic activity, but her occasional roles in small theater companies and her printed stories in pulp magazines are only part of her life. She represents art in its proper focus, and as such she seems the most obvious spokesman for the general beliefs of the author. Neither she nor the author would accept the idea of art for its own sake. Norah is too much interested in people for such a selfish attitude.

Under her influence Philip sees Hayward in a new light. It is five years now since they met in Heidelberg, and Hayward is getting older without having accomplished any of the great designs of which he spoke so glowingly in Europe. In fact he has not even set out to accomplish them. He is more than ever the symbol of the artist misdirected, and it seems that the author spares no pains to show how weak he truly is. An example of this is the situation in which Hayward is offered a position as a critic for a newspaper, and which he rejects because it would interfere with his "inner life." Of course he deceives himself into accepting this point, and he tries to explain the offer away with vague references to forthcoming books which demand his attention. But by this time Philip is aware that Hayward will never fulfill any of his wishes and dreams. Hayward is incapable of contending with the world in its reality and on its terms.

At this time Philip uncovers another friend. It is the very popular Griffiths, who is some years ahead of him in the medical school. When Philip is ill, Griffiths aids him with untiring devotion. Philip has won a new friend, and it is not often that such a thing happens to him. Thus, things are much more cheerful in Philip's life. Norah, his success at school, and Griffiths all now made life much more peaceful. But as usual the author is not going to let Philip rest in his new surroundings.

Comment: These chapters simply form an isolated moment of relative calm. The greatest disaster of

all, the most trying one is still to confront Philip, and Maugham, as a good technician, does not want to show his hero as going from one crisis to another without some measure of peace and contentment.

OF HUMAN BONDAGE

PART TWO

· ·

OBSESSION: CHAPTERS 69–78

Sadness comes back into Philip Carey's life when he opens the door of his rooms to find Mildred waiting for him. The surprise is literally too much for Philip to accept, and he flounders under the weight of its impact. He is stunned. His first reaction is to ask what she is doing there, and the impact of his surprise is voiced very gruffly to Mildred. But his anger soon turns to sorrow and love as Mildred relates her sad tale of her life with Miller. As Philip again reacts to the presence of Mildred the author reminds the reader of the irrationality of love. Philip has been much better off without Mildred, he has had peace and contentment with Norah, but he soon returns to his old position of a worshiper at Mildred's shrine and soon involves himself in the same depths of obsession and depression.

Now the truth of Mildred's relationship to Miller comes out. They had not married, primarily because Miller was already married. But the fruit of their affair is a child which is to come to Mildred in a few months time. And Miller has now abandoned her and returned to his wife. With the circumstances clearly in his mind, Philip is surprised to find that Mildred was so wanton and reckless in her love for Miller. But he cannot help taking her back.

W. Somerset Maugham makes the reunion scene between Philip and Mildred quite ironic. She accuses Miller of being cheap and of telling her lies, but she is only accusing her lover of the same evils which she has done herself. Maugham also points out that there is a parallel in the passion which Mildred felt for Miller in the passion which Philip feels for her. The **irony** further continues in the fact that Mildred is now willing to marry Philip, and that he is disgusted by her sensuality. Yet this does not diminish his own desire for her - it simply makes him fully aware how foolish marriage would be to a woman like Mildred.

Mildred's entrance again also introduces a problem for Philip in the person of Norah. He had been happy in his relationship with Norah, but now he must try to break off from her without hurting her too much. As usual, Philip does more damage when he tries not to hurt someone than most people could do intentionally. He tries to avoid Norah, and starts arguments with her when he does see her. He refuses to see her so that he can be with Mildred, but Mildred makes another appointment, so that he is left alone. Finally Norah comes to him and Philip tells her that Mildred is back. In a very touching scene the author paints for the reader the picture of despair on Norah's face as she hears that Mildred is taking her place, and again the idea is suggested that love is not called for and it does not come when we ask. It comes in the most unusual and strange situations and plagues man as much as it pleases him.

Norah departs and Mildred moves back into the heart of Philip. She moves into an apartment which he provides for her, and the merry-go-round of frustration soon begins again. Mildred soon becomes a great expense to Philip (naturally she is above asking Miller for any money). It is apparent that she has counted on Philip's help, and that she has made all the arrangements for the birth of her baby. She soon returns to her composed manner and assumes the role of middle-class respectability which is ever her ideal. Again the author adds a touch of **irony** to show how very shallow Mildred is, for she is a great fan of Norah's and reads the inconsequential novels of Norah with great appreciation.

Eventually the time comes for Mildred to have her baby. She has concocted her story to cover her position, and she is quite concerned to make a good impression at the hospital. Of course this costs Philip more money, for she needs the best doctors and the best care available. But for all the money spent to insure the safe delivery of the baby, Mildred is not particularly concerned if the child lives or dies. The author gives that impression that Mildred would be quite relieved if the child died. At any rate she does not want the child to live with her, and before she is born the mother is already making arrangements to board the baby with a "respectable" woman.

A girl is born and the birth of her daughter brings out some of the humanity of Mildred. She finds temporary contentment in her period of recovery and even offers some love to the child and to Philip. But Philip is more happy over the birth of the child than is the mother, and he offers to take all three of them on a vacation to the beach resort. Soon they are off to Brighton (where Mildred lived with Emil Miller), and they have the prospect of a peaceful vacation before Philip returns to his studies. At the resort Mildred's attention is directed to the pleasures of the midway and the ease of summer sun. She is indifferent to the baby, and it is evident that Philip is more concerned with the tot than the mother. The author seems to emphasize the fact that the maternal instinct is dead in Mildred, and she even becomes jealous over Philip's attention to her daughter.

Philip cannot spend all of his time at the shore, so he leaves Mildred there with the child. He has work to do at his hospital, and he is preparing for a difficult examination. He does pass the examination in which most of the others are failed, and he writes of his joy to Mildred. But she is as selfish as ever and her answer says nothing of the success. Instead she writes to request more money, this time for a new hat so that she may impress the people of the boardwalk. Her letters seem to reflect so much joy in new-found friends at the beach that Philip is afraid that he would be in her way there. It is often in such a situation in the relationship between Philip and Mildred that the author will develop another problem for them to face and wrangle over. Here, however, the author surprises the reader by again allowing Mildred to come out of her selfish role and assume the guise of humanity. Unbelievably she greets Philip with genuine joy when he comes to see her again at the resort. Of course Philip is surprised by her greeting, and overjoyed too. It is this occasional balance in the personality of Mildred which makes her acceptable to the reader, for if she were always so selfish and vulgar, she would be unreal.

At the shore Philip again spends a great deal more money that he anticipates. However, he is caught up in the mood of summer fun, and his remark in answer to Griffith's question if he can afford the extra cost is quite typical of thousands of vacationers: "I can't, but what do I care." Philip is happy for the moment, and he shares his joy with Griffiths, who has become a dear friend by this time. Philip has told Griffiths of Mildred, and he feels that they are similar in many ways. He feels that they could be friends - and knowing something of the make-up of Mildred by this time the reader might very well sense that this is the creation of a situation which Philip will regret.

The shore is quite joyful for Philip and Mildred and her daughter. They enjoy the luxury of good restaurants and the ease of life in the sun. Mildred almost becomes happy as she promenades with Philip on the boardwalk, and Philip feels that she is coming to love him. He has the idea that they should go to Paris for a weekend, and that there he will finally be able to have the physical satisfaction of Mildred's love. And she is not averse to going, even though she protests of the decency involved. The Paris trip becomes quite important to Philip and he plans the details with great care as they are coming back toward London. And Mildred is quite interested in Paris by this time.

But Mildred's interest in Paris is soon replaced by her passion for Griffiths as she meets him on her return with Philip from Brighton. Griffiths is introduced by Philip and Mildred sees that the new man is quite attractive and she is immediately drawn to him - with something like the same passion which Philip feels for her. Griffiths is quite the contrast of Philip in very many ways. He is handsome, gay, and outgoing - the life of the party in every way. And more, he is nearer completion of his course than Philip, so he has more immediate prospects for a good living. In short, Mildred is interested.

Soon after they meet the two are quite friendly. He calls her Mildred and she addresses him as Harry, and she takes the liberty of inviting him to dine with them. Ironically, Philip is quite pleased that they have taken to each other so quickly, and again this shows his innate simplicity and goodness. He cannot imagine that they would be so much attracted to each other that they would betray his friendship. Philip is sure of Mildred by this time, and he feels that her love will be his if only he can be patient. But Mildred has other ideas.

One night as they are all dining out Philip begins to realize that their conversation is only directed to one another and that he is excluded from their conversation and their thoughts. He is hurt deeply, but his pride will not allow him to make a scene. He purposely goes away from the pair so that they can speak easily, and he stays away to show his indifference to the situation. But of course he is not indifferent - his heart is pounding with jealousy and anger. Philip gets into such a fit of emotion that he is miserable company and he is rude to both Mildred and Griffiths. He is in the center of despair. He knows he is losing Mildred and there doesn't seem to be anything he can do about it.

As they leave the restaurant and hail a horse-driven cab Philip is in agony. But again W. Somerset Maugham will not allow the situation to resolve itself without a particular twist which shows his artistry and his knowledge of human nature. As soon as they get into the carriage Philip is startled to find that Mildred slips her hand into his. It is such a simple gesture and Philip is overcome by happiness. Now he repents for thinking that Mildred was preparing to betray him for Griffiths. In a few seconds how changed he is. This gesture, he is sure, is the final step to assure the fact that she does love him and not Griffiths. All is right with the world. All the effort and financial sacrifice have been worth it. She does love him. He is so happy. And then he notices that Mildred is also holding Griffith's hand!

The fact brought physical pain to Philip. The suffering was intense. Yet, he could not allow them to know how he felt, and he went on talking as though nothing had happened. Here the author raises a poignant question through the actions of Philip.

It is related to the fact of man's conformity to proper decorum and the rules of social conduct. Philip is in spiritual and physical agony, but he will not admit it. He leaves his two friends alone, knowing their physical attraction to each other. Philip reveals something more of his masochistic tendencies; it is as though he received some pleasure from the sadness and perversion of the situation. Moreover, W. Somerset Maugham seems to be asking if there isn't something of this desire to suffer in all of mankind. It is a question which is answered in the affirmative in this novel, as Philip Carey's subsequent actions will show.

After Philip and Griffiths take Mildred home, Philip asks his friend if he is in love with Mildred. Griffiths shows some of the fabric of his personality when he emphatically denies that he cares for her and makes a joke of the entire situation. For the moment and for the next day Philip is overjoyed by his answer, but he realizes how much Griffiths has deceived him soon enough. Philip intentionally does not see Mildred the next day, since he wants to demonstrate his independence from her, but Mildred is not home fretting about his feelings. She and Griffiths have had lunch together and they have mutually declared their great passion for each other. The revelation of this fact cuts Philip to the quick. Griffiths has lied to him, for within minutes after Griffiths declared he had no love for Mildred he was writing her a note declaring that same love. Philip is startled by the infamy of his friend. He will never see Griffiths again.

By this time in his young life Philip Carey is used to pain. One might say that he lives with it. He accepts the betrayal by Griffiths and Mildred almost stoically. It is again reflective of the masochism in Philip's nature. But this masochism is not planted in Philip accidentally by W. Somerset Maugham. The author realizes that Philip's actions will exasperate most of the readers of this novel, but he also realizes that it will intrigue them. This explains his concentration on the details of Philip's internal agony as he prepares to help his former friend and Mildred to realize their sexual hunger.

The extent of Mildred's sexual desire was never as vivid to Philip as it is in her relationship with Griffiths. Philip had been able to dismiss Mildred's affair with Emil Miller as a mistake and a product of his deception that he intended to marry her. But now the physical attraction is obviously the only point of emphasis for Mildred. In his full realization Philip realizes what a fool he has been - but that is not going to prevent him from being a fool again.

Philip does emerge from his lethargy for a few pages in the novel, especially when he boldly confronts Mildred and calls her a liar. He will not accept any more of her tricks; he wants to beat her; she owes him everything. He calls her a vulgar slut, and she responds with a familiar attack that she never liked him and that she only used him for his money. Then to show her consummate gall she hands Philip a bill for a new dress. He tells her to pay it herself, or to get Griffiths to pay it. He knows that Griffiths has as little money as she. And when she asks for money to go home in a cab he tells her to walk. He refuses to pay any more. All of this shows Philip in a more virile role than one is accustomed to, and his manliness looks good on him. One might stand up to cheer his independent attitude. But again the author brings out the essential humanity which governs all of Philip's actions when he allows himself to slip some coins into Mildred's hand to use for the cab. Philip's period of independence is short-lived.

If Philip had been more independent he might have avoided the spiritual agony of the subsequent events in his life. But the next day Mildred comes begging to him, proclaiming that she realizes that she must give up Griffiths. Her utter despondency moves Philip, for she soon breaks into tears and tells Philip of her great passion for Griffiths. The scene is filled with great **irony**, for before long Philip is trying to console her over the situation. If one could be entirely unconcerned he might add "what fools these mortals be," but the author is certainly not unconcerned. W. Somerset Maugham allows the reader to see that Mildred's passion is just as great as Philip's and that she can no more control it than he can. Philip sees this too, and in one of the strangest **episodes** in any novel ever written Philip insists that he will pay for the trip which Mildred and Griffiths want to take together. It is an act born of perversion and despair. It violates every concern for decency and it seems to be inspired by insanity. But it is also typical of Philip. He is going to give them money so that the sensual appetite may be appeased and so that when it is all over Mildred will return to him. The result of this pact between Mildred and Philip is expected to give her a weekend of love and him the peace of her love when she returns (she does promise to go to Paris with him). She kisses Philip in gratitude! Finally, after some reservations on Griffiths' part, both he and Mildred depart for their weekend of love, leaving Philip in the solitude and despair of his own room. He theorizes that they are both quite common people and that this is the cause of their attraction, and the reason why he offers the money to them is the fact that he wants them to debase themselves completely. Of course his actions again demonstrate the masochism of his own personality. He seems to glory in the act of his own debasement. He is as low as he ever was in his entire life, and somehow he is to exist through the weekend until Mildred comes back.

Philip becomes morose from the great boredom of his room, and he turns to drink as an outlet, and then to a common prostitute. He seems to relish the sordidness of his own perversity. Again there is the touch of **irony** in the prostitute using the same words of Mildred in accepting Philip's attention: "I don't mind" rings through his ears with the sound of her voice.

Finally Monday comes, and Philip waits for the opportunity to visit Mildred in her rooms. He still wants her at any cost. But he is disappointed on Monday, for Mildred has not returned. Nor does she make her appearance on Tuesday. Philip is going crazy as he waits for her. His misery is compound by a letter from Griffiths which begs Philip's forgiveness, but Philip cannot be bothered now or ever with the man. His attitude is that one should not apologize for evil, especially when one has given himself so freely to it. But philosophy will not bring Mildred back.

On Wednesday Philip runs to Mildred's rooms, only to be stopped by the landlady who informs him that Mildred has been back and has gone for good. As usual Philip hides his emotions, but again his heart is rent, and he realizes that Mildred never had any intention of coming back to him. It was all a ruse to get the money, and then to disappear. Her promises of a trip to Paris were only other examples of her gross lies. With this realization fully before him Philip thinks of suicide as an outlet from his misery, but here his native intelligence takes over and assures him of the stupidity of the act. He knows that he loves Mildred and that he has a great deal of suffering to go through before he can erase her from his soul, but he knows that time will heal all wounds. It is a sign of the maturity which Philip is winning. Maturity is expensive, but apparently it can be attained, and then there will be no more hurt from love.

Philip retreats from London to spend the summer with his uncle in Blackstable. There he gives himself to reviewing the situation which caused so much anguish in his life. He comes to the conclusion that these experiences are necessary, unavoidable even, and that one cannot define them. One can only respond to them and wait until the pain is gone. He realizes that desire is impossible to define, it can only be felt. And in this light Philip was more sure than ever that men were beasts, and that they were driven by forces over which they had no control.

Philip's second sequence of obsession for Mildred had made him more of an animal and less of a man in many ways. He found himself groveling before her, and he consented to acts which would startle the most debased mind. The philosophy of indifference and resolution which he had tried to adopt had not worked. Not at all. One positive point was that it was over. He was thankful for that.

Comment: The startling events in these chapters speak for themselves, and the meaning lies in the intense pain which Philip inflicts on himself as he descends into an inferno of perverse passion. He is now truly in bondage. Even so, the greatest torment is still to come, for we realize psychologically that Philip has not really paid for his faults in the transaction with Mildred and Griffiths.

PROGRESS AT SCHOOL: CHAPTER 79-81

Philip Carey returned to his studies at medical school with a sense of joy. He knew that if he could immerse himself in studies and work he would be able to forget Mildred more easily. But he does not want the same apartment as before, so he moves his belongings to a new four-room flat. His possessions still include the Persian rug which Cronshaw sent him from Paris, and the riddle of its meaning is still bothering him.

In setting up his new life Philip cannot help but include something of the past. One remembrance he has is of Norah Nesbit, and one day he goes to visit her. He had found peace with her in between the agony of his life with Mildred. But Philip's design of a new start with Norah is defeated when she announces that she is engaged to be married. Again Philip feels that he has missed an opportunity for happiness, and he is ashamed of the way he treated her and of the way he comes now to beg some pity. Norah is as ever a decent and refined person - an ideal wife if he could love her and have her. But he did not truly love her, and he will never have her. When he leaves Norah's rooms he realizes that his vanity is hurt more than his heart. The gods have played a joke on him, and it is surprising to see him laugh along with their humor.

The other remembrance is of Mildred, and it is Griffiths who brings her to mind again and again as he begs Philip to see him and to forgive him. But Philip will do neither. And perhaps there is some justice in the way that Griffiths is forced to put up with the advances of Mildred long after his own passion has subsided. He ends up evading Mildred at all costs and even has his housekeeper call a policeman so that she will leave his doorstep. On this touch of **irony** the second **episode** of existence with Mildred Rogers fades from Philip Carey's life.

Philip is assigned as an out-patients' clerk at the hospital, and as such he comes to see the somber side of city life. He is under the supervision of Dr. Tyrell, a good man who has made his success in the world the hard way. The doctor's attitude is rather gruff, but he is quite a humanitarian at heart, as he demonstrates to Philip in his concern for the sick and by his advice to the young interns. In the job Philip encounters all the members of London's poorer class, as well as some people who are better off but who pretend poverty so that they may be treated free. Perhaps because of his own deformity, and perhaps because of his pleasing and sympathetic manner, the people take to Philip quite easily, and he finds great joy in comforting their needs. He is on the road to becoming a good doctor, and there is much wonder in him. He again reflects on the fortunes of life, and comes to the happy thought: "perhaps I'm cut out to be a doctor. It would be rather a lark if I'd hit upon the one thing I'm fit for."

The implication of W. Somerset Maugham's novel is that it is quite a "lark," for Philip is quite fortunate to find that all of his earlier errors may now be erased by a life which provides a good living and a sense of accomplishment. Slowly Philip acquires the sense of dedication which his profession requires, but it is difficult work in many ways also. Every day Philip saw men and women walk in off the streets to be told that they are going to die, and there is nothing science can do for them. The poor are never able to afford the rest homes and the best medicine, nor the specialists. Moreover, they can't afford to stop working. What the author seems to be emphasizing here is the great need for getter services for the poor, and as such his novel was a forerunner to the great social developments in medical service in England and in America in the later decades of the twentieth century.

Work in the hospital provided a perfect cure for Philip's great despair over the loss of Mildred. He was able to patch up his heart and make it so strong and durable that one might never know it had broken.

Comment: This represents another interlude. The structural pattern of the novel alternates such interludes with crises which become progressively worse, until Philip reaches the very depths and

barely survives. But here, for the moment, Philip is reasonably content. Probably Maugham uses this principle of structure because it leads to an increase in verisimilitude: we become convinced that life is accurately reflected in his work.

CRONSHAW: THE DEATH OF A POET: CHAPTERS 82-85

Philip had always been intrigued by the riddle of the Persian rug which the poet Cronshaw had told him, and he is delighted to hear from his friend Lawson that the poet is now in London. Naturally he goes to find him, and he does, in the filthiest corner of London. The poet has returned to England to die. He is still a heavy drinker, and he will not give it up even if the alternative is a coffin.

Conshaw's point is that he has lived his life the way he wanted to do, so there is no need for any change now. He regrets nothing in his life, not even his death. He only hopes that when the moment comes he can be as strong and as unrepentant as he is now. Again there is reference to the Persian rug, but Cronshaw still refuses to tell Philip the answer to the riddle. The poet says that "The answer is meaningless unless you discover it for yourself."

There is some alteration in Cronshaw's attitude though, for he has decided to publish his poems. He still maintains that there is no public for poetry and no fame in it, but he has found a critic who likes his work and the latter has arranged to have the volume put in print. He is only consenting to have it published now because he wants to leave something behind, no matter how inconsequential, which will allow the world to remember that he was a part of it.

Cronshaw's physical condition is so desperate and his financial condition so poor that Philip insists that the poet come to live with him. Philip has an extra room which is not used, and the old man would hardly eat much, so there was no great cost involved. But there is a person who makes the situation difficult, and this is Leonard Upjohn, the critic who has found Cronshaw's work worthy of publication.

Upjohn at that time was a rising critic, and there is much to recommend the man for his effort to publish Cronshaw's work, but there were other designs in his mind also. The point is that he is an opportunist who is using Cronshaw's volume to push his own reputation. Philip finds him unbearable, for he realizes that the man Cronshaw means nothing to the critic Upjohn. Upjohn seems to resent the fact that Philip took Cronshaw out of his filthy room and put him into clean sheets. It would be much more poetic to the critic if the poet died in his garret.

Again in these circumstances W. Somerset Maugham must be reflecting upon the attitudes of art which are so removed from the assets of humanity. Upjohn is quite content to allow others take care of Cronshaw and to provide for his wants, but he wants to present the poet's art to posterity. But in this situation there is so much that is shallow and so much that is selfish. It is the old question of the value of art, the same question which the author introduced when Philip was a student in Paris. Again W. Somerset Maugham seems to be emphasizing the fact that there are important things in this world beside art.

Finally Cronshaw does allow Philip to bring a doctor to see him, but only because of the possibility that Philip could have trouble with the authorities if the poet died without a doctor's care. Of course Upjohn is against it, and he accuses Philip of a lack of "delicate feelings." This cuts Philip to the core, for the very reason why he has taken Cronshaw under his care is his great concern and feeling for humanity. Finally, Dr. Tyrell of the hospital does come and he informs the young student that the poet may die any minute. Cronshaw takes the news with resolution. He will not do anything to help himself.

Cronshaw's efforts would probably have been in vain anyway. He died the next day in his sleep. And thus Philip found himself at another funeral, and he found that his money would bear the great part of the expense. The undertaker would take care of the details with "Economy, Celerity, and Propriety," and Philip was left alone with the corpse of his friend. Upjohn was busy with friends and was unable to make an appearance until the following day, but when he did arrive he had much to say regarding the funeral arrangements. It was easy for him to decide; he wasn't paying a cent. The critic felt that the poet ought to be set to rest with great pomp and circumstance, and when Philip refused, the critic refers to him as cheap and narrow-minded.

The author seems to be making the point that Upjohn has no real feeling for Cronshaw, and that even while the funeral procession is moving toward the grave the critic is thinking of the preface which he will write to the poet's poems. Whatever the critic does to distinguish the ceremony is only artificial, as exemplified by his insistence that they place a wreath on the fallen poet's head, much in the manner of the ancient Roman legionnaires. But Philip will have none of it. He is much too engrossed in the presence of death all about him. The death of Cronshaw reflects the futility of life, for in spite of his last minute grasp for immortality in his poems, it would not matter to the world that he had ever lived. Also, the death of his friend causes Philip to re-evaluate his own philosophy of life, for his relationship to values and the policeman around the corner had not brought him any assurance.

Following Cronshaw's death his book of poems does appear, and Upjohn does write an effective review of it for the leading newspaper. But he borrows something from the poet's license for exaggeration as he places himself in a much better light and accuses Philip of being quite callous about the fate of the great poet. It is a gem as literature - but it is not true. Again, W. Somerset Maugham is questioning the values of critics and artists in a society which apparently is not going to be moved by either. Again the point is that life has dimension beyond art, and art is not going to satisfy the inner spirit of man completely, no matter how sweet its song. Upjohn has had his victory for the moment. But it is short-lived - about as permanent as the daily paper he wrote in.

Comment: These brief chapters deal with the relationship between art and life once again. Despite Philip's speculations, we are convinced that Cronshaw's life has meaning, and that the artistic creation which involved him throughout that life has some measure of validity. We are not so certain about Upjohn, for it would seem that he and his kind are another of the professions or fields of life which Maugham satirizes in the novel, and which he finds to be futile. Upjohn has, as far as Philip is concerned, even less to offer than Mr. Carter's firm of accountants.

FRIENDSHIP: CHAPTERS 86–89

In the midst of his relations with Cronshaw, Philip was offered a possibility that his club-foot might be corrected somewhat. Dr. Jacobs, the assistant surgeon at the hospital gives him his first real hope in years that something can be done, and of course

Philip's emotions are quite elevated. He begins to look forward to the day when he will be nearly as normal as everyone else. It is somewhat reminiscent of the time when Philip was very young and he asked for a miracle to help him. Now he does not need the miracle, he only needs science and money.

As he continues his training Philip becomes an in-patient clerk for six months and he works in the wards. Again he is quite successful in his relations to the patients, and he makes a particular friend in Thorpe Athelny, who is ill with jaundice. Philip is attracted to the jolly man who is full of adages and humor at every turn. Athelny is a press representative, and he has had a most interesting life. He is greatly devoted to Spanish art, and it is through Athelny that Philip is introduced to the paintings of the Spanish mystic El Greco.

Athelny obviously has a good background and education, and it surprises Philip that he must rely on the charity of the world when he enters the hospital. But in back of that is a long story, and again it pertains to values in a world which has too many distorted ones and too few honored ones. W. Somerset Maugham paints Athelny as a renegade from wealth and a happy man in poverty. He was once married to a wealthy woman, but she stifled his individuality and made him into a carbon of herself. Finally Athelny revolted and ran off with the cook, with whom he has lived for nearly twenty years, raising nine children, and finding happiness. All of the children are illegitimate in the eyes of the world, but there has never been more of a legitimate father. He loves his children dearly, and his affection for his wife has not cooled through the years.

Philip finds Athelny such a delightful person that he is happy to accept the man's invitation to his home. Philip arrives on the next Sunday and meets Mrs. Athelny and the nine children who cluster about at home. It is a delightful situation for Philip, for he never had any brothers or sisters of his own, and he has long forgotten the warmth and affection of a family grouped together. A touch of humor is always Athelny's stock in trade. Thus his wife is called "Marie of the soapsuds," and each of the children has as unusual a name as that. Some of Athelny's philosophy of life soon gets to Philip, and he begins to reflect upon the wisdom of his new friend in relation to his own life. Athelny tells Philip never to marry a woman as smart as he is, for a man does not want a wife who is his intellectual equal. Athelny believes that a marriage is happiest when a woman knows her place, which is in the kitchen or taking care of the children. *chauvinist*

In many ways Athelny reminds Philip of the poet Cronshaw, and it is possible that the author is introducing Athelny to reflect a contrast in values. In many ways both men are the same, but Athelny is alive and happy in his circumstances, while Cronshaw was always miserable. The distinction between the two seems to have been that Athelny was able to ward off the blows of life with his humor and ease, while Cronshaw found life sad and uncomfortable. If Cronshaw had a little bit of Athelny's nature he might have been a greater poet and he might have lived.

Life in Athelny's household is unusual in many ways. In spite of the fact that she is not legally married to her husband Mrs. Athelny has always remained a loyal Christian, and both she and her husband have reared the children in religion. It is ironic that there can be spiritual values in such circumstances. But Athelny will not accompany them to services, and his attitude may reflect the belief of many people in our day. He says that the services are beautiful, even if they are not true. This reflects much of his concern for art, especially the art of the Catholic Church in Spain. As such he says that he believes that religion is only a part of man's temperament, and that many people do too much to formalize it He is concerned for morality even if he has lost a religious basis for it.

Athelny is given to long reminiscences of his years in Spain, and Philip eagerly listens to the older man's tales of Spanish art, music, and religion. Philip is again intrigued by Athelny's description of El Greco's art, and when he sees some reproductions of the Spaniard's work he is sure that there is something great there. It reminds Philip of his days in Paris and it recalls the search that his friend Clutton was making to find the release for his soul.

Philip has found a sympathetic soul for the future, a friend who can be counted on. He is already indebted to Athelny for bringing him to the threshold of a great discovery regarding El Greco, and he shall have many other opportunities to express his thanks to him again. Athelny has given support to Philip's rejection of the ideal in this life, for idealism is not consistent with the life around the world. As such Philip develops his attitude of **realism** and objectivity more than ever, but he still cannot understand nor explain the depths of his philosophy. He had learned long ago in Paris that art was not involved with beauty nor ugliness, only with truth. But truth had been hard to discover in the jumbled world of emotions and passions which dominated his soul. He was thankful to Athelny that he had again pierced his soul with the discovery of El Greco. It seems to mark a return to the concerns of the spirit for Philip Carey, and as such it is all part of the maturing of the boy into the man.

OF HUMAN BONDAGE

TEXTUAL ANALYSIS

PART THREE

OBSESSION: CHAPTERS 90–97

Philip had found great joy in the household of the Athelny family. He soon came to respect and love each member of the family and he was truly happy in their surroundings. He was a weekly visitor for Sunday dinner, and there is even the hint that young Sally might one day be the girl for Philip to marry. But W. Somerset Maugham does not allow either Philip or the readers to live long in ease before he reminds them that life is full of its valleys and mountains. Philip is now moving down again. Mildred is coming back.

Appropriately, one night as he walks home from the peace of Athelny's home he sees Mildred, and his life is turned to torture again. He had not even thought of her for weeks, but when he saw her he had to follow her. And soon Philip's torture is turned to horror as he realizes that Mildred is now a prostitute. As soon as he confronts her he knows that she is going to become a part of his life again, and within a few days she has moved into his rooms and into his life, along with the child of Miller. But the situation is not exactly the same as it was before, for Philip has lost all romantic attachment to Mildred and he is only aiding her as a friend and out of attachment to the child.

Once inside Philip's rooms Mildred loses the rudeness or crudeness of her ways and she assumes the guise of middle class respectability as she poses as Philip's wife. For the present she is quite content to serve Philip his meals and to rest after her ordeal on the streets. She has been made quite low in her experiences, and the author may be trying to evoke some pity from the reader as he shows her better side. What is more obvious though, is that the author is again experiencing his mastery of plot structure and character development. Again he is giving Mildred something which will appear to be humane and which will appeal to the reader's emotions. If he did not inject this humanity the reader could not allow her a place on the page, and this would be disastrous for the novelist.

When Mildred enters into her third sequence with Philip he makes it clear that any former love he had for her has gone. He cannot explain why it is no longer there. It just isn't. He wants to help her in her present situation, and there is something akin to a religious devotion in his actions. His actions are certainly good and they are done without hope of reward or desire for revenge. Thus there develops a point of contradiction in Philip's actions and his ideals. For he has tried to argue that there is no need for idealism in this world, but his very actions refute the point. Philip represents the confused state of mind of many young men who try to find a new philosophy to govern their actions, only to find that they must rely on accepted values to direct their lives.

After Mildred has been in residence for a short time there naturally develops the fights and arguments which have punctuated her association with Philip since they first met. She feels that she can still dominate Philip by his love for her, but Philip is not the same man he was before and his feelings can never be rekindled to the state of ecstatic passion she once knew. He is no longer attracted sexually toward her. He doesn't know why, but it is all over. And he is thankful for it.

But Mildred is not content with the situation. Time and time again she refers to their situation as unnatural, indicating that it would be preferable to live in sin than to live without it. Mildred is humiliated by Philip's lack of concern and it takes her quite some time to fathom the extent of his withdrawal from her. And the ease which Philip finds the need to withdraw only increases her anger. Often Philip is so engrossed in his studies or in the world's affairs or in the company of his friends that he has little time to spend with Mildred. He usually dines with her and then sits down with a book for the evening. At other times he leaves the apartment and meets his friends for a night of discussion and drink. But, Mildred is generally excluded from that life.

Mildred rebels occasionally and berates Philip for treating her as his servant. It is certainly not Philip's intention to do so, but on the other hand he is quite careful not to start any relationship which will draw him to her again. On one particular occasion Mildred waits up to entice Philip, but he dismisses her curtly without giving the idea another thought. Naturally she is more upset than ever, and as her passion grows so does her anger.

Soon enough Philip also realizes that he has miscalculated about the cost of Mildred and the little girl in his life. Both of them need clothes occasionally, and the food bills are much higher as Mildred is not adept at making last night's meat look good in a new setting. She is a poor housekeeper and wastes money without realizing where it has gone. Two cannot live as cheaply as one and three simply multiplies the error.

In his weekly meetings with Hayward and Lawson, Philip is introduced to a man who has some inside tips on the stock market. This is Macalister, and in the process of the months Philip becomes rather friendly with him. He wants Macalister to watch out for something good for him on the market, and he is greatly disappointed when all of his friends make a good deal of money on a tip from Macalister at a time when he wasn't able to meet them. Their gain is his loss, and it merely whets his appetite for the next possibility of speculation on the market. Philip needs the money for Mildred and her child, but he also secretly longs for some extra cash so that he might have Dr. Jacobs operate on his bad foot.

Finally the opportunity to invest does come and on his first venture into the complicated world of stocks Philip emerges the victor. He is able to sell his shares for a thirty-pound profit and his first thought is to have the operation on his foot at the next school vacation. His second thought, appropriately enough, is to buy some new clothes for Mildred and the girl and to take them all for a holiday to the shore. As usual Philip is not selfish with money and he shows an awareness of the problems of others. It is also quite obvious by this time that he is quite taken by the child and that the reason why he bears so much of Mildred's ill feelings is because of his affection for the little girl. It is a situation which Mildred soon realizes and which she tries to take advantage of.

Philip's operation puts him in the hospital for a month, and in addition to helping him physically and mentally the operation may also help him professionally, for he understands that the average person would not have much faith in a doctor who was not whole himself. It is an interesting point that the author does not spend much time in writing of the effect of the operation on Philip. The reader presumes that Philip is aided and that he will be able to walk better from this time. But it is not a complete cure.

Part of the rest period is spent on the seashore. But Philip insists on two rooms for the three of them. He does not want to allow himself the temptation of Mildred's love, and as such he brings her to tears in rage. Mildred expresses her displeasure with: "I might be poisonous." Her remark is a good indication of Philip's feelings for her, and she is humiliated by his lack of passion. In a typical passage of **irony** in the novel she asks Philip what people would say about a man not sleeping with his wife, and it is so appropriate for Mildred to think about "people" and not the true point of morality involved in their relations.

Life in the boarding house is interesting to Mildred though. It gives her an opportunity to exchange lies with the other guests. She invents preposterous stories of her background with Philip, and assumes the guise of a lady who demands every respect. But to Philip she is as dull as ever with her lies and exaggerations. As such Philip finds that he is extremely bored with Mildred, but he cannot leave her. He longs to visit the Athelny's at a nearby resort, but he feels that Mildred would humiliate him. With the full realization of how low a person she is, he wonders what madness made her so desirable before. The answer is inexplicable, but Philip feels very fortunate that he never married her. That would have been the end of his life, but now he feels that it is only just beginning. He wants to travel after his medical studies are over, particularly to Spain. There he can see the El Greco paintings which have intrigued him so lately, and from Spain he can venture out into the rest of the romantic world.

Philip's dreams are cut short when it comes time to leave the seashore and return to his studies at the hospital. But Mildred feels that her vacation is just starting - at least she is not interested in getting a job very soon. She is quite content to live off the goodness of Philip, and she finds every excuse to avoid taking any job. She had been waiting for the fall season to find a suitable position, but now it was nearly Christmas and she was still taking her pose looking at the want ads in the daily paper. Christmas still finds Mildred without work, but it does find Philip in the spirit of the season, and as such he tries to make the holiday pleasant for all three of them. It is a pleasant scene by normal standards to see a man and woman and a child together at Christmas sharing in the joy of the moment. But it is a scene choked with suspense when it involves Philip and Mildred. Surprisingly enough peace does prevail through the holiday, and Philip does kiss Mildred good-night (on the forehead), and in the calm light of the moment Mildred again seems quite normal and decent. By this time the reader may begin to remember that with Mildred there is always the calm before the storm. And the storm is about to begin.

Mildred becomes more upset by what she considers Philip's unnatural attitude toward her. He is completely indifferent to her, and this is what irritates her. She cannot realize that Philip does not love her anymore, and she feels that he is only trying to hide his passion. He will not listen to her mean remarks and he is not as attentive as he was before. She becomes jealous and imagines that he loves someone else, but of course she is wrong. It becomes an obsession with Mildred to have Philip love her again, if only for the joy that she can have by refusing him. But Philip is not interested in her at all. He is attracted to the little girl, Mildred's tot, and in her anger Mildred sees that she can still hurt him through the child.

In the depths of Mildred's frustration the child becomes a symbol of what she is to Philip; since he loves the baby, he puts up with her. In her mind she begins to long for freedom from the situation, but as she is so dependent upon Philip she must swallow her pride. She begins to panic, because she knows that she cannot contain her rage much longer. In her confused state she even begins to believe that she loves Philip and that if she would bear his baby he would be tied to her forever. Her obsession grows with his indifference, and one night she determines to see the situation through to its conclusion, no matter what.

The scene which follows is one of the most dramatic in the entire novel, for when Philip comes in from his night with his friends Mildred attempts to seduce him. She positively leers at him, and it is as disgusting to Philip as it is to the reader. We now see Mildred in her entire baseness, and her passion is completely spent. At first Philip is surprised by the extent of her sensuality and he sees her in a better perspective than ever before. But Philip cannot be excited, his passion has long been worn out, and the only way he can react is to reject her advances as nicely as possible. This only kindles her passion more, and when she sees that Philip is not going to fall into her trap she becomes a raging animal, spitting out filthy words and vulgar expressions, ending with the vilest epithet she can think of - "Cripple!" In this memorable scene W. Somerset Maugham has allowed Mildred to show her full colors and from this point she cannot win the reader's nor Philip's sympathy again. And if there is any doubt of this fact it is resolved the following day when Philip returns from his duties at the hospital to find that his apartment has been completely demolished by the maniacal actions of Mildred. She tears and batters and scars and mutilates every piece of Philip's furniture and books and his keepsakes. In her frenzy she forgets to destroy his clothes, but they are the only things which are left.

Of course Mildred is gone in the wake of her wreck, and Philip is happy to be rid of her. His only pensive thoughts concern the child who will have to be reared by such a mother. He is so relieved to be rid of Mildred that he cannot feel any anger toward her. He feels that he will never see her again, and that this is the end of her invasion into his life. He is nearly correct, but not quite so.

Ironically, one of the things which Mildred destroyed in her rage was the Persian rug which the poet Cronshaw gave to Philip. It was still an interesting and challenging thing to him to discover the meaning of the riddle of the rug, but he would have to solve it without the rug itself.

Comment: With this scene, Philip's passion has burnt itself out. Whatever may trouble him in the future, it will not be the hopeless longing for a quite unworthy object. But Philip has yet to pay in full for his obsession.

POVERTY AND DESPAIR: CHAPTERS 98–101

After the agony of his life with Mildred and her eventual disappearance, the reader might expect that Philip Carey's fortunes might look up. But W. Somerset Maugham has other plans as he traces the adventures of Philip through a hostile world. The author seems intent upon showing the reader what the depths of despair and poverty are like. Moreover, he seems to imply more than ever that they are interwoven. Philip is about to enter into the final two years of his education, but this part is not in the clean atmosphere of the hospital, it is in the squalor of the slums. It is an education which will make Philip into a man - or turn him into an animal.

The fall for Philip starts rather pleasantly. He has made some money through his friend Macalister on speculations on the stock market, and now he would like to make one more gain to compensate for the expenses of his last involvement with Mildred. His hopes are high, for Macalister explains that a rise is bound to come after a long siege of war and an eventual armistice. Philip agrees to the venture and puts most of his money into it. He hopes to sit back and wait for the war to end and for the profits to come in.

But the war does not end, instead it takes a turn for the worse and the price of his stock declines daily. The war has changed many things and many lives and all of its casualties are not on the battlefield. Philip is a victim at home. As the stock prices drop he loses nearly every cent he has, and he is reduced to a poverty he has never known before. Somehow he is able to bear the loss before his friends, and he pays Macalister every cent.

In his despondency Philip tries to enlist in an Army contingent which is going to fight, but he must stay at home because of his clubfoot. His friends generally avoid the fighting, but quite mysteriously Hayward does enlist and is soon off to the battle. Philip had lost most of his respect for Hayward by this time, and he was quite surprised by the action. Hayward had always taken a superior attitude in life, and patriotism to a cause or a nation was not one of his assets. However, he is becoming older now and he has not fulfilled his dreams of literary greatness and artistic individuality. His enlistment seems to be his last chance to win back his own integrity; if he can't live well perhaps he can die well. It is thus that W. Somerset Maugham puts this vacuous character in his best light in the entire novel. The reader has found Hayward a selfish and egotistical person throughout, and, as Philip, he has realized that Hayward's greatness was never to be realized. But now the author presents a side of the man which was not shown before, and when he sets off to fight his country's battle it is indicative of the fact that there is something decent in the worst of us. Of course Hayward was not to find praise on the battlefield. He never won a medal. He never had a chance to. He died of disease, not of wounds. His death was a far better thing than his life. But Philip was not to realize the completion of his friend's sacrifice until he had been through another type of battle himself.

The money that Philip has left after his stock losses is soon spent. He cannot pay his room rent, and he cannot get help from anyone. His uncle the vicar positively refuses, and his friends have been similarly affected by the bad war news. He does borrow a small sum from Lawson, but he doesn't spend it, for he wouldn't know how to repay it. He sells everything he can get along without, and tries to get any kind of job in medicine so that he can stay in school. But the gods are against him and every effort fails.

Rather than face his landlady after promising her money for the back rent Philip leaves his room and goes out into the city to find some way out of his problem. He becomes one of the many homeless men who wander through the streets of London trying to find some sort of job to hold themselves together. He meets the side of London society which he has never known, and he becomes a part of it. He becomes one of the men on line waiting to be interviewed (and usually rejected) for a job. He sleeps in the park and on benches and eats scraps for his meals. He comes to know poverty in its rawest sense, and it is a tribute to his tenacity that he does not sink into the depths of despair. He is held up by the fact that he cannot fully comprehend the enormity of his own situation. He feels that it is either a bad dream, or that he will be rescued by some hand of goodness.

But the hand is slow in coming. For a week Philip prowls the streets of London, searching for some port in the storm which has become his life. He felt that regret was absurd, for it did no good, and by this time he was reasonably sure that what had happened was pre-ordained. He could not pray - there was no God to pray to. His last coin was spent on the day that he usually went to see his friend, Athelny. It would also be his last day if Athelny could not help him.

Life at Athelny's was the same as ever, but Philip was too ill and too tired to enter into their happiness. He put on a brave front, but was too sick to eat the dinner he had been thinking of all week long. But here W. Somerset Maugham allows Philip some ease after his ordeal on the streets, and it is Athelny himself and his family who come to Philip's rescue. Athelny had been concerned when Philip didn't come the previous week and he sought the man in his rooms. The landlady told him all he needed to know. Thus Athelny proves to be the source of relief which Philip needs so desperately, and in this regard Philip realizes how good the man is. He may not be a practicing Christian, and he has nine illegitimate children, and he is not a success in the eyes of the world, but he has more goodness than his uncle the vicar, and he has a greater concern for his friends than Lawson and Macalister have shown.

Philip has found his port, but the storm is not over.

Comment: Maugham is making a particular point about formal versus actual moral goodness as he draws the character of Athelny. For Athelny is formally a sinner, yet he shows more humanity and compassion toward Philip than do his, Philip's, own blood relations such as his uncle, who is a clergyman into the bargain. It is clear that Philip would have died were it not for the generosity of Athelny.

THE WORKING WORLD - II: CHAPTERS 102–108

W. Somerset Maugham makes it quite clear that Philip's life is saved by the generosity of the Athelny family. Philip had known for long that people seldom kill themselves over love, but suicide is often considered a good escape from poverty. He had used his last coin to get to Athelny's home - it was the coin of hope. If Athelny had turned him away Philip would not need a coin to take him away. Death could be found easily enough.

But now such thoughts were dispensed with for the moment. He had the love and the comfort of the Athelny's and he had his friend also in the search for a job. It came rather quickly, but it was hardly what Philip expected. With his education and intelligence he hoped for something in which he could display his talents. But the only job was as a floor-walker at a large department store - the same one for which Athelny worked - and he had to accept the position. And he was lucky to get it, he realized, as he recalled the numberless men whom he met in his futile quest for work.

Soon Philip realizes the terrible boredom of the average person at work, for he is only required to direct people to particular departments in the store and it is dull and repetitive work. His job requires long hours and he must stand all day. And when work is over there is not a very pleasant prospect in store for him, for he must live at the company's quarters and sleep in the same room with three others. Thus the job does provide him with a little money and his daily bread and his nightly bed, but it is oppressing too. He cannot have a moment alone, for from the time he is propelled from bed in the morning until he creeps back into it late at night he is in the public eye.

Comment: In many ways this picture of life reflects the naturalistic school of fiction which was generated in the latter half of the nineteenth century. Naturalism tried to give a picture of life in great detail and it generally over-emphasized the negative side of man's existence. However, W. Somerset Maugham is not concentrating on the negative approach only; he is merely using it as a device to show what demands are made upon the poor. Their lot seems unchanging and they are often enough satisfied with what they have (perhaps they are happier than the rich), but they are too often the pawns of unscrupulous men of business. The point of irony is also introduced again, as it runs through so much of Mr. Maugham's fiction. In order to get his job Philip must obtain (actually borrow the money to buy) a formal dress suit, and he must wear it every day in order to make his place in a world of squalor.

To his surprise Philip does rather well in the business world. He is generally accepted by his fellow workers, even though he finds it hard to share their likes and dreams. He goes to the monthly dance given by the store for the employees, but he is socially misplaced and physically incapable of joining in the activities. The girls there might have an interest in him, but he has no interest in them.

Philip's first payday comes and he earns 18 shillings for a month's work. On today's market a shilling would be about fourteen cents in American money, but it was worth something more than. It was worth his life, for it kept him from dying. It was horrible to think that he would have to spend so many more months in this store, doing the same thing day in and day out. His only hope was the inheritance he expected to receive at the death of his uncle. Soon he begins consciously to wish for the death of the old man so that he might spend his young years in peace back at the hospital and later in practice. Philip is in his late twenties by this time and his uncle is forty years his senior. The younger man wants to get a hold of life; the older one wants to hold on to it. If Philip could pray he would pray for a severe winter of cold and rain. His uncle's poor condition was sure to kill him if it came.

Philip's fortunes in the store are raised quite unexpectedly by a call to decorate the main windows. It is a mortifying assignment for him, for he expects one of his friends to look in any moment, but he is successful and wins the applause of the store's buyer. Soon Philip is given similar assignments and his talent for art and design take him off the floor to the back of the designer's studio. Life is a little bit better for him, but it is not happiness. He has climbed from the pit of despair in which death was a solace until life was at least bearable. But this type of life brought him too close to humanity in the raw and he was ready to look on every one with suspicion. An example of this occurs when he accidentally meets Lawson on the street. Lawson is quite civil and concerned with Philip's plight, but Philip cannot forgive Lawson for not aiding him when he needed it so badly. Life's progress had driven them apart and he did not want to try to regain the past. The past was over, it was best to forget it and the people in it.

But certain people defied forgetting. Hayward had resigned himself to failure and died in war uselessly rather than go on. Cronshaw had lived a failure and wanted to find success at the last minute. Life had no meaning and Philip asked himself: "What is the use of it?" Suddenly he realized the answer to Cronshaw's riddle. The answer was that life had no meaning, and that it doesn't matter what a man does on this earth, for his epitaph will only read the same as everyone else's: "He was born, he suffered, and he died." It was an important realization for Philip and he felt that it gave him the answer to everything which had ever plagued him. Since there is no need to care for anything Philip felt that he was finally free. He had found that freedom he went searching for when he left King's school fifteen years before. But again there was **irony** and agony in the realization that whenever he found the thing he was searching for he also found that it brought him little of the peace he was seeking. Philip found that the idea of happiness was the last illusion, and he had to throw it away. He threw happiness away and he was happy for the moment.

Philip moved up to a position as a dress designer for Mr. Sampson, and he won some local fame by designing a dress for an actress to wear in a musical comedy. But the work is never satisfying and he only waits for his uncle to die so that life can begin again. The uncle is obstinate and refuses to die to accommodate Philip. On his trips back to Blackstable Philip sees his uncle suffering and alone, and he realizes that his uncle is kept alive at great expense by the local doctor. Here it is interesting to question whether the author is pointing out the incongruity of keeping the man alive with drugs when he is only a few steps removed from a vegetable existence. Uncle

William, the vicar, can never recover, as the doctor knows well, and it may seem useless to many to keep him alive. Certainly it does to Philip at this time, for the uncle's death will mean freedom for both of them: Freedom from pain and freedom from poverty.

But Uncle William has more at stake than Philip and he wills to stay alive. He knows where he stands on earth and in spite of his life in religion he has some doubts about his place in the next world. He has hopes of living to the age of some of the patriarchs from the Bible. Philip realizes, however, that there is a serious concern on his uncle's part about salvation and the beliefs of religion.

The two weeks of Philip's vacation are spent and he has to return to his position at the department store. His life there resumes in misery, and all of his dreams are about his uncle's death. He constantly thinks of Spain and his desire to see the paintings of El Greco. He studies all the backgrounds of Spanish life, and tries to learn the language and to read *Don Quixote* in the original. He is constantly rejuvenated in his desire to see Spain by Athelny, and they spend hours planning Philip's tour down to the last detail.

Life at Athelny's home also provides Philip with some interesting experiences. Sally is growing up, and she and the other children are starting out in life in menial and common jobs, but they seem quite content with their lot. Mrs. Athelny also provides a bit of food for thought when she contradicts her husband's enthusiasm for life. She feels that her sacrifice for her children is too much and that if she had to live it all over again she would not marry. As such she is made to represent many of the masses who find that their lives have not had fulfillment -

and as such she coincides with Philip's philosophy that life has no meaning.

Again, it is worth commenting that no matter how differently the Athelny's feel about particular questions, they do agree on the love for their children. Perhaps Mrs. Athelny might want to do something else in another world, but W. Somerset Maugham seems to convey the impression that she has had a full life this time at least. And Philip Carey's life is fuller, too, from his association with the Athelnys.

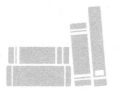

OF HUMAN BONDAGE

....

OBSESSION: CHAPTER 109

Although Philip has not attended the medical college for nearly two years he occasionally returns there to pick up some mail. On one visit he sees a letter from Mildred in his box. He hesitates to pick it up, for he knows it may mean that he will become involved with her once more. But again his basic decency comes through, for he feels that Mildred may be in great need of help.

The reader might well ask why she is allowed to intrude upon the story again, but her re-introduction is again an example of the artistry of the author. Mr. Maugham wants to tie up some loose ends in the novel, it seems, and he wants to give a candid view of Mildred's new life. Philip does read the letter and after some soul-searching he goes off to Mildred's room. She is living in the lowest section and she is still in great need of money. She had anticipated that Philip would be a doctor by this time and in a very definite way his visit is intended to be professional.

Mildred has contracted venereal disease and she is again living the life of a prostitute. Her daughter is dead. Philip remarks that the child is better off. Mildred is not particularly *uh* sorry, for her life is hard enough as it is. As usual, Mildred can present herself in a good light in the most adverse conditions, and it is a question whether the reader can allow himself any pity for her. Certainly Philip has little pity by this time. But he does try to help Mildred. She says that he is the only friend that she has ever had, and she invites him out to dinner as her treat. In one of the most telling moments of the work Philip answers "All right, I don't mind." He is using the very words which she used to him so many times in their early courtship, and there is more than a hint that by this time Philip has something of the hard-heartedness of the woman. It is almost as though he caught the disease from her.

But Philip can never be as hard as Mildred. He tries to help her and gets a prescription. He is completely bored by her at this time, but he would do as much for a sick cat. In the days that follow he realizes that Mildred really hasn't changed much. She doesn't want to work, and she continues to lie to him. She swears that she is through with her life on the street, that her illness has changed her completely. But Philip soon suspects that she is as active as ever in her trade despite his advice, and one night he follows her as she begins her rounds.

When he confronts her she is ready to pour out her abuse upon him, but she realizes it will not work. He tells her that what she is doing is criminal, but she saunters away from him into a theater and it is the final act of Mildred in the life of Philip Carey. The reader is left with the impression that Mildred will work at her profession until she dies. Her disease has already taken its toll and death is already setting into her cheeks. Philip is happy that it is all over.

Comment: Here the fire of passion is gone from Philip. There may be a little too much melodrama in the fate of Mildred: a diseased prostitute moving ever downward to her inevitable sordid end. But Philip still pities the woman, and does not take any satisfaction in seeing her who had so cruelly used him in turn undergo her own punishment.

THE DEATH OF THE VICAR: CHAPTERS 110-112

On his Christmas holiday Philip went down to see his uncle the vicar. He was drawn for two reasons: to get away from the crowded room and to see if there had been any change in the old man's condition. He found his uncle very bad, but the old man was not ready to die quite yet. Uncle William is taken care of by a good woman, Mrs. Foster, and he dominates her much as he did his wife. But the woman cares for the old man with great devotion.

At this time Philip also notes that his uncle looks upon the advent of death with even greater horror than before. Philip wonders if the old man can still believe the doctrines of his own faith, for the vicar seems intent upon prolonging life at any cost. Cost becomes an important word here, for Philip begins to think that it is unnecessary to take the expensive drugs which keep the old man alive. Philip is concerned that there will not be enough for him when his uncle is dead. As such he begins to look and feel like a ghoul waiting at the grave for his uncle to fall in. Unconsciously he finds himself appraising the value of various pieces of furniture which can be sold. For one bizarre moment he even contemplates murdering the old man.

It is thus that a man can be driven by poverty and despair. Philip has always been a good person, but now he contemplates the most hideous crimes in order to free himself from poverty. He tries to view his uncle as he was earlier in life, and Philip thinks that the dying man was always mean and insensitive and horrible to his wife. Philip cannot feel any sorrow for his pain, but he cannot kill him either. Ironically, the uncle wakes when Philip thinks of killing him, and intuitively the vicar knows what has been on Philip's mind.

The vicar hangs on to life with a firm grip and Philip hangs on to his job until the time when the uncle slips. Finally in July, two years after his great loss on the stock market, Philip receives the call that the old man is dying. He leaves the department store with great speed, but it is not the great joy he expected. Somehow he had become attached to the people in the store, and he had come to sympathize with their problems. For two years he has been waiting for the moment to fly away, but the satisfaction he receives is never as complete as he originally believed. He has found that life is much this way, and he is to add to his knowledge as the years go by.

Uncle William ends his life living on drugs. One night as Philip sits by his side Uncle William calls for the solace of Communion and admits that he is going to die. The final event brings some compassion for his uncle to Philip, and in this mood he witnesses the final minutes of his only living relative. Uncle William takes the Communion and receives the spiritual strength to make the long trip out of life. It is a marvelous change for the uncle and a surprising moment for Philip. *chills*

The suggestion here may be that the uncle was hesitant about dying as it meant that he would be confronted by his wife again, and that she may be there to accuse him of many evils in his life toward her. Now he is sure that she forgives him and he is ready to make his way to her. Soon Uncle William takes his last breath. It is a beautiful day outside and Philip realizes that the old machine was run-down.

Philip received everything his uncle left. It came to over five hundred pounds; it was enough to allow him to finish medical school. His only remaining job was to dispose of the vicar's effects, and in the process he reads a letter written by his own mother when he was born. It is a poignant letter, and Philip realizes how much different he is than she hoped him to be. It is sad, but there is nothing he can do about it. When his job was done Philip left Blackstable to take up residence at the hospital again. He was nearly thirty. All of his friends had succeeded and were settled in life. At least now he was back on the right track.

> **Comment: Philip was not in any danger of seriously entertaining the thought that he would murder the dying man to hasten his departure. For Philip is simply not that kind of man, and besides, his training as a doctor has been to preserve life. He withstands temptation here without the support or the standard of a firm religious faith, and it is possible that Philip's natural goodness, like Athelny's, is really the subject of this section, as much as is the Vicar's departure from life with its dividend of rescuing Philip from his servitude.**

END AND BEGINNING: CHAPTERS 113-122

After his uncle's estate was settled Philip Carey was able to return to medical school to finish his course. He had one year to go and after graduation he intended to fulfill his dreams by visiting Spain and then spending a number of years as a doctor on ships sailing throughout the world. He had received the desire to go to Spain from Athelny, and he had been influenced toward travel and foreign places ever since he was a child.

Philip's final year at the hospital is spent in great ease and without the frustrations which formerly beset him. He spends a period in maternity work, and he becomes a great success in his relations with the poor. He has every reason to understand their plight. It is a somber scene which the author paints for Philip, with the squalor and filth of the slums as a background for his work, but Philip is happy helping others. He sees life and death all about him, and he feels a fulfillment in his work.

Much of Philip's free time is spent with Athelny and his family. After his uncle's death Philip brings them all presents to serve as thanks for the time that they saved him from suicide. He is quite content in their company, and he arranges to spend his summer vacation with them. The family has replaced all of his former friends in his affection, and he has lost much of the interest in art which dominated his earlier life. He sees the children growing up and preparing to go out into life on their own. He watches Sally mature into a lovely woman, and his eye is taken by her simple beauty.

Philip receives his diploma in August. He is nearly thirty years old. He is getting a late start, but fortunately there is work immediately available, and a day after graduation he is on his way to work for a doctor in a seaport village. He becomes the assistant to Doctor South for the summer period, and with Dr. South he receives the practical experience necessary to become a good doctor. Again, the common people take to Philip, and where others have failed he wins the respect of Dr. South. Life in the village appeals to Dr. Philip Carey, and when Dr. South asks him to become a full partner in his practice Philip is quite honored. But he cannot accept. It would mean the end of his dreams of travel and of foreign places. He had been instilled with this desire by Athelny and others and he wanted to find the freedom and joy of the world after being confined by circumstances and his own personality for so many years. He leaves Dr. South's village, and the doctor tells him that the offer will always be open.

Philip spends his vacation with the Athelny's on the Isle of Thanet. The entire family spends the holiday there picking hops, and they have the double advantage of basking in the sun and making some money, too. The Athelny's are happy as usual, and the sun gives a radiance to all of them. It particularly nourishes the beauty of Sally, and Philip is taken back by her resemblance to the Greek beauties of his literary studies. He feels that there is more of the beauty of ancient Greece in the bronzed beauty of Sally than in all the history books.

One night when he and Sally are out on a walk Philip is overcome by the perfection of the world of nature and of Sally's relation to it. His senses have been excited by nature in full bloom and in a moment of passion he takes Sally as his mistress. It is almost as if they became a part of nature itself when they became lovers. In the magic of night, love is complete.

But the world of the morning is another situation. Philip regrets his moment of passion and feels that Sally will hate him and be ashamed of herself. But Sally is too much of nature's child to regret her actions, and she accepts Philip with little more than the ordinary decency which she has shown him over the years. Philip feels that he does not love Sally, not as he loved Mildred at any rate, but he does respect the nineteen-year-old girl for being such a "splendid animal." She is an example of nature functioning perfectly.

But nature's function cannot be throttled, as Philip soon discovers. Sally thinks that she is pregnant. It comes as a terrible shock to Philip, for if it is true it will destroy all the dreams which others have built up for him and which he now wants to come true. He knows he will marry Sally if she is to have a child, and it shows the essential goodness of Philip. He realizes that other men might abandon the girl, but he is too decent for that. The Athelny's have become his closest friends, he couldn't abandon Sally to take care of a child alone (certainly he must be thinking of Mildred's daughter here), and after all it would be his child, too. Then Philip begins to reason that he must prepare to take care of his future family, and he writes to Dr. South that he will accept the position at the seacoast. He resigns himself to the new life which he will enter upon as a husband and father, and he feels that it is not too bad after all. After all, he will have the sea at his door, and he can share the travel stories of the seamen as they dock. He remembered the words which the poet Cronshaw had told him years before: "...the facts of life mattered nothing to him who by the power of fancy held in fee the twin realms of space and time."

Philip realizes that he wants the life by the sea with Sally and their child. He longs to touch the perfect feet of his child, and he feels that he will be a good parent. His own deformity has made him a better man than many others, and while it has taken away some of the physical activities of life, it has compensated by giving him time to savor the beauty of art and nature - and people. His hurt and anger about Mildred and Griffiths are gone. He can pardon those who have hurt him. Life is not without meaning; there are values and beliefs. There is faith.

The final scene of the novel is set in the National Gallery, where Philip has agreed to meet Sally. His life is fuller now and he can view the great paintings in a better perspective than ever before. As such, art supplies a background for his life, but it is not out of proportion. Sally comes in, and Philip can hardly wait to tell her of his arrangements for the marriage and their future together. However, Sally startles him by announcing that she is not pregnant after all. This is another touch of W. Somerset Maugham's talent, for all of Philip's preparations were unnecessary. He still can go on his trips, he has nothing to bind him to England or to that seashore practice. He can travel the world and enjoy all the things which others have described so vividly. Their world is opening widely for him to enter it.

However, in a moment of great revelation Philip Carey realizes that the world the others have painted for him is not his world. He wants the world by the shore, not on the sea, and he wants Sally and his son to share it with him. He had never followed the desires of his own heart before - it was always the advice of others. Now he will be his own master finally, and he wants simplicity. The simple life is the most perfect after all. It means the end of all of his dreams, but reality may bring happiness more than dreams.

And Philip will be happy, the reader is assured, with Sally. He asks her if she will marry him. Her answer at first is reminiscent of Mildred's "I don't mind," for Sally says it is time that she was settling down. Philip asks her again, if she wants to marry him. All of his frustration of the past is wiped away by her answer: "There's no one else I would marry." Her words complete the beauty of the final scene in this novel. The sun is shining, and Philip is beaming. Life has been cruel at times, and most generous at other times. The past has come to an end, the future is just beginning.

OF HUMAN BONDAGE

. . . .

SALLY ATHELNY

She is the daughter of Thorpe Athelny and his common-law wife. Sally is a young girl when the reader meets her in the novel, but in the course of the action she matures into a beautiful woman. She is portrayed as a child of nature, and she has all the freshness of the great outdoors. This is particularly evident at the close of the novel when she and her family and Philip Carey are on a combination holiday and money-making trip to the English countryside. Sally is a city girl who blossoms in the country and as such she becomes a personification of her father's ideals about living the life of nature. Also, she is in many ways a distinct contrast to Philip Carey's other great love in the novel, Mildred Rogers, for the latter is fragile and sickly, with a yellowish complexion, while Sally has a rosy outlook in her physical appearance as well as in her outlook on life. At the close of the novel Philip Carey proposes marriage to Sally, and as such W. Somerset Maugham allows a "happy ending" to compensate for the generally miserable existence which has plagued his hero.

THORPE ATHELNY

This man comes into the life of Philip Carey while the latter is working as an intern in a hospital and while Athelny is recuperating from an illness. They soon become friends and this allows the author to offer Athelny as a solace to the general sorrow which fills Philip's life in his late twenties. It is Athelny who takes Philip into his home when the younger man is on the verge of suicide. As such he presents Philip with a new view of life's mores and its morals, for Athelny was once a man of wealth and prestige, married to a woman of property whom he hated. Now his situation is altered completely, but most important he is quite happy with his common-law wife and their nine children. As such W. Somerset Maughan seems to use Thorpe Athelny as an example of man undominated by the false standards of goodness in the world. Just as his wife and, particularly, his daughter, Sally, Thorpe Athelny becomes another symbol of man living in accord with the designs of his nature.

MRS. THORPE ATHELNY

This woman is not legally the wife of Thorpe Athelny, but she is the mother of his nine children. She is a woman from the lower classes of society, and as such she is contrasted with Thorpe's legal wife, but W. Somerset Maugham takes great pains to emphasize the fact that she is a much better person at heart, and that she too is living in accord with the designs of nature. She seems to represent the basic goodness of the common person, and much of her goodness rubs off on her daughter Sally. There is a point of coincidence in her relation to Philip Carey, for she was born and raised in the same area as he and she is shown to possess much of the same basic goodness and devotion to her husband as Philip's own Aunt Louisa. Here the contrast begins and the **irony** of their relationship is obvious, for Aunt Louisa was the wife of a clergyman and therefore quite respectable, while Mrs. Athelny would be considered by society to be living in sin. She is a hard-working and long-suffering woman who adds happiness to her home.

PHILIP CAREY

Philip is the hero of this novel, but he is a different hero than many others in the world of fiction. The novel traces his life from the time that he is a young boy until he is a mature man of nearly thirty. He is presented as a person with "two strikes" against him from the start, for he is both an orphan and a cripple. These two forces do much to dominate the personality and, thus, the life of Philip Carey, and most of his anguish and sorrow can be traced to them. But his "strikes" also add something to the adult man whom the young boy becomes, for Philip realizes very early in life the negative forces which are found in the world and as such he is accustomed to them long before most boys ever feel them. Philip does have some compensating factors as well, for he is essentially a very intelligent person and he is talented in the world of art. It is his reason and his intelligence which carry him over the hardest part of his life when he is penniless and nearly defeated in life's struggle for existence. *Of Human Bondage* also stresses Philip Carey's relationship to Mildred Rogers, and as such the author gives the reader a startlingly accurate view of the obsession which can dominate a person in the throbs of passion. Indeed, passion is the right word to describe the relationship between Philip Carey and Mildred Rogers, for love is certainly not involved. Love is made of much finer stuff, but passion is represented as course and brutal and frustrating. The feeling which Philip has for Sally at the end of the novel is love, and it contrasts sharply with his feelings for Mildred.

WILLIAM CAREY

This is Philip's uncle, a vicar in the Anglican Church. The vicar is portrayed in negative terms throughout most of the novel, and is shown to be a narrow-minded person who has few of the qualities which his own faith would require. As such Uncle William seems to be the butt of W. Somerset Maugham's attack upon accepted social and religious values. The study of the life of William Carey might be contrasted with that of Thorpe Athelny, for the latter is not a member of any church and he is living in a marriage which has not been blessed, but there is an essential goodness and understanding of and compassion for mankind in Athelny which the vicar does not have. Indeed, up until the time of his death the vicar is viewed negatively by both Philip Carey and the reader; yet near the close of the book W. Somerset Maugham does portray the vicar in something of a positive view. It is as though Uncle William had finally realized the hypocrisy of his life and that he had confessed his unworthiness and made his peace with his Maker.

MRS. WILLIAM CAREY

This is Philip Carey's aunt and the wife of the vicar. In many ways she is the opposite of her husband, and the contrast emphasizes her positive value. She is essentially a good woman and she aids her nephew in many ways. She loves Philip as if he were her own son, and in many ways she thinks of him as the son she never had. It is Mrs. Carey who brings a little light into the dark boyhood of Philip and it is she who allows him to pursue his career as a painter in Paris. Over-all, she represents the positive side of the religious question which the author introduces throughout the work.

CLUTTON

Philip Carey encounters Clutton when they are both art students in Paris. Clutton is the most talented of all of the students with whom Philip comes in contact, and he has a dedication to his art which matches his talent. In many ways he is Philip's ideal for a time, but in the process of time he is forgotten. Yet, there is something memorable about Clutton, for W. Somerset Maugham presents him as the true artist who is functioning in his chosen field. Here Clutton is contrasted with Philip and Flanagan and Fanny Price, who are, in various degrees, incompetent artists. Clutton seems to represent what is positive about the arts and their demand upon the artists. In the hands of a gifted person all the effort is worthwhile.

CRONSHAW

This is another character whom Philip Carey meets in Paris. He is a poet and a philosopher, and not very successful as either. When Philip is in Paris Cronshaw intrigues him with his riddle of the Persian rug, and for years it is a problem which vexes Philip. Later Cronshaw does come to London and there he lives and finally dies in the apartment of Philip. In essence the author seems to portray Cronshaw in positive terms, but he is a man who lives and dies for negative causes. An example of this is the fleeting fame which comes to Cronshaw after his death when his poems are published. They do create a stir for a short time, but in a few months they are in the second-hand shops and the author is forgotten. It is presented as a sobering thought for the potential artist who would devote all his life to his cause. The author seems to say that life has other considerations and dimensions than the world of art.

FLANAGAN

This young man is an American art student in Paris who is there more on a vacation than as a serious art student. He has some talent, but he is not obsessed with art, and he does not suffer the same dismal fate as Cronshaw and he does not sacrifice his talent for financial reward as does Lawson. He also seems to be presented as a balancing factor between the positive dedication of the creative Clutton and the negative obsession in the talentless Fanny Price.

FOINET

He is an art critic and teacher in Paris. He is not a very successful painter himself, but he does have an eye for the value of the work of other painters, and as such he ekes out an existence. It is Foinet who helps to direct Philip Carey away from art, and the boy is eternally grateful for saving him from a wasted life. It is almost as if W. Somerset Maugham were saying that Foinet wished someone had done a similar favor for him many years before.

GRIFFITHS

This man is a fellow student a few years ahead of Philip Carey at Medical school. He is hale and hearty and often the life of the party, and in many ways Philip is envious of him. Griffiths is often used as a contrasting factor to the life of Philip Carey, and it shows how poorly Philip is adjusted to society. It is no wonder that a woman like Mildred Rogers would be stirred to passion by Griffiths, for he represents what is sensual and accepted in a world which has closed its eyes to the value of the soul.

HAYWARD

This is Philip's friend throughout most of the novel. He is a talented person, but he is too much of an artist and not enough of a person to be a success. He is a person who is always dreaming of success, but the author makes it clear that it is only a dream and that Hayward is not doing anything to put it into effect. He is always referring with a certain amount of mystery to his new book and to his new ideas, but Philip Carey and the reader are both soon aware that Hayward's talent will forever remain unfulfilled. Towards the end of the novel there is a strange development in which W. Somerset Maugham allows Hayward to alter the course of his life by enlisting in the army during a crucial period. The result of his enlistment is death, and it is not a death filled with glory; rather, Hayward is cut down by sickness and hardly receives a notice in the press.

LAWSON

Philip Carey encounters Lawson while both are in Paris as art students. Lawson has more talent than Philip and he does find some commercial success as a portrait painter later in life. Yet this is a compromise to his early standards, and it seems that the author uses Lawson to represent the artist who would prostitute his talent for money. Philip's decision to forget art is viewed as more admirable in this respect, and as the years go by the former friends have little in common and drift away completely.

MACALISTER

This is a stockbroker who has a great effect upon the life of Philip Carey, once in a positive and once in a negative way. Macalister is a rather shallow person who seems to live by gold alone, and he helps Philip invest in poverty. Macalister obviously represents the interests of "big business" in the world of Philip Carey, but it is a world much too complicated for Philip's understanding. That is why after a fortunate circumstance of a small profit from an investment Philip is later rendered penniless from a disastrous adventure on the "market."

EMIL MILLER

Emil is Philip's rival for the love of Mildred Rogers. Actually, the reader never meets Emil in the pages of this novel, but he does make his presence known. Emil is pictured as quite the opposite of Philip Carey - strong and virile and somewhat vulgar - and as such he is attractive to a woman like Mildred. After an affair with Mildred, Emil leaves her alone to bear their child and he rejects any responsibility for taking care of the child when it is born. In every respect he seems the opposite of Philip Carey.

NORAH NESBIT

Norah becomes Philip's solace after Mildred runs off with Miller. Philip finds peace with Norah, but he does not love her as she loves him. Norah is the intellectual equal of Philip, and she represents the artist (in this case a writer) who knows her limitations. As such she writes for a particular class and she has a facility of writing rapidly so that she may earn enough to keep herself and her child alive. She seems far removed from the ideals of Hayward in this manner. Norah, however, only proves to be a fleeting part of Philip's life, for when Mildred returns Norah is forgotten.

MR. PERKINS

This man was Philip's headmaster at prep school, and it is he who first recognizes Philip's talents. Perkins encourages Philip to develop his abilities and as a teacher he presents quite a contrast with the usual authoritarian teacher whom Philip meets at school. Yet, Philip's relationship with Mr. Perkins is not entirely beneficial for both of them, for the teacher fails to keep the boy at school and on his way to the university, and the student fails to follow the wise advice of his teacher. When Philip re-visits his school many years later he realizes how correct the headmaster was, but he cannot erase the years as he could a blackboard.

FANNY PRICE

This woman loves Philip when they are students together in Paris. Fanny represents the untalented artist who wastes her life on art. Art is her life, however, and when she fails there is no other alternative but death. As such she represents a point of view which runs through the pages of the novel that art must be subordinate to other more important values, and that one must never sacrifice his humanity for the sake of art. Fanny deteriorates as a person because she wants too much from art. It seems to be the point of W. Somerset Maugham that most people will never find what Fanny sought, and that it is better to admit defeat than to strive forever without success.

MILDRED ROGERS

Mildred is one of the most evil women in all of modern fiction. She comes into Philip's life while he is studying medicine and she proves to be the worst thing for him of all the evils he encounters. Almost from the time of her entrance Mildred dominates Philip's life, and she brings out the worst in him in every way. Mildred is a proud, selfish, slovenly, vulgar person, and one would have to search for an evil which she does not represent. Yet, Philip Carey feels that he loves her and he is willing to go to any end and through any means to possess her. Of course his idea of love is only passion, and in the process of the story he does come to realize how low Mildred really is - but it is an interesting question whether he ever fully loses his passion for her. The author seems to allow Mildred to represent the women who pose as cultivated and demure while they are coarse and sensuous at heart. At the end of the novel Mildred has become a prostitute and she has contracted the disease of her trade. She is dying and she doesn't seem to care - at least she will do nothing to stop her decay.

ROSE

This is Philip Carey's boyhood friend. He is the opposite of Philip in many ways, but as many opposites they are attracted to each other - at least for a while. When the inevitable break comes it is Philip who suffers the most, for Rose is able to win friends quite quickly, but Philip is ever silent and usually alone. Years later when Philip re-visits his old school he thinks of Rose with sadness, but there is **irony** in the fact that he can't remember his old friend's name.

DR. SOUTH

The doctor is an interesting picture of a gruff man with a heart of gold - his bark is far worse than his bite. Philip comes to assist Dr. South during the busy summer after the young man has been graduated from medical school, and in the course of events the older doctor offers the younger one an opportunity to take over his practice when he dies. Dr. South has been through most of what Philip dreams about-far-away places with strange-sounding names - and he represents the sober side of life in contrast to the visions which Thorpe Athelny generates in Philip. When Philip finally accepts Dr. South's offer to share his practice it represents Philip's final realization that life's values are closer at hand than the islands of the Pacific.

EMILY WILKINSON

Philip Carey encounters Emily Wilkinson in his first love affair. She is much older than her lover, and there is something pathetic in her need for love from Philip. But to Philip it is all a lark - at least at first - and he is overwhelmed by the idea of conquest in his first encounter with a woman. However, Philip soon tires of Emily and he has a difficult time evading her. It is interesting to note that Emily had the same type of background as Philip, and that she too rebelled against the authority of her faith and her family. Again, W. Somerset Maugham seems to be questioning the values which the older generation was imposing upon the new.

OF HUMAN BONDAGE

. . . .

There seems to be little room for a middle position among contemporary critics concerning Maugham. His readers have been lavish in their praise of most of the short stories and at least four of the novels he has written. But there is nothing like that uniformity in the critical commentary which has been written. And there has not been a great deal written. It seems that W. Somerset Maugham was one up on many of the critics when he wrote his *The Summing Up*, in which he tells of his own life and the background of his literary efforts. Hence he has discouraged many would be biographers and literary investigators who could twist his stories about his life and get some point of order from their own distortion.

Mr. Maugham finds a space in every critical review which has been written in the past thirty years. He is there in snips and snatches, generally, and seldom in depth at all. Two of the more important hooks for courses in the English novel on the college level have been quite miserly in space or critical development. One of the more successful texts for colleges, *Cavalcade of the English Novel* by Edward Wagenknecht, refers to W. Somerset Maugham in about one-half of a page, and it mentions books by the author rather than explaining them. He is mentioned one time in the text proper, and then only as a follower of Samuel Butler in style and mood. *The English Novel* by Walter Allen offers not quite three pages and makes some negative conclusions which seem quite excessive. Mr. Allen does admit that Mr. Maugham is "an admirably professional writer whose strength...has come from his knowing perfectly his own limits." The critic accuses the author of working "in a very narrow range of subject and character, without any compensating quality of style to make up for it." The same critic finds *Of Human Bondage* "one of the most moving accounts of loneliness in our language," but he is not at all satisfied with the ending. Mr. Allen finds the last part faked: "Sally, the girl with the placidity and acceptance of an earth goddess, never becomes credible, nor does her father, Athelny." He continues that the Athelny family is "carefully planted where it is in the novel to make a happy ending seem possible...their appearance flaws the novel as nothing else."

To balance these two somewhat negative evaluations of the author have come two books in the last five years which show the other side of the coin. The first, *W. Somerset Maugham: A Candid Portrait*, is by Maugham's old friend Karl G. Pfeiffer. Professor Pfeiffer is on the faculty of New York University, and he had known Mr. Maugham for thirty-five years when he wrote his biography in 1958. The book is essentially a tribute to the author's friend, and as such Mr. Maugham comes out quite agreeably. It is full of anecdotes and acute observation, and its purpose seems to have been to entertain rather than to inform. But it is an essential work for understanding the personality of W. Somerset Maugham. Professor Pfeiffer seems to have picked up more than a knowledge of bridge in his thirty-five year association with the famous author.

The second book with positive evaluations is *Somerset Maugham: A Biographical And Critical Study* by Richard A. Cordell. Professor Cordell was on the faculty of Purdue University when he wrote his book, and he did quite a bit of research into the early life of W. Somerset Maugham. As such he was able to erase many myths which had built up around the author's earlier years and his life at medical school. Professor Cordell makes much of the influence of Naturalism in Mr. Maugham's work, particularly stressing the influence of Emile Zola on Liza of Lambeth and subsequent novels. It is Professor Cordell who tells us that W. Somerset Maugham has still another important work on his life tucked away in a corner of his home at Cap Ferrat in France. However, neither Professor Pfeiffer's work nor Professor Cordell's work has had too much of an impact on the scholarly evaluation of W. Somerset Maugham. Those who like the works of the author are content to enjoy them and allow the critics the doubtful pleasure of evaluating them.

Dr. Carlos Baker of the faculty of Princeton University has given the works of W. Somerset Maugham a higher position than many of his colleagues. This critic finds the author is "a writer riddled with critical barbs who deserves something better at our hands than he has ever received." It is Dr. Baker who has emphasized a point of value in Maugham's work which is essential in understanding the author's outlook. The point of value is Mr. Maugham's emphasis that writing and art are not the only important things in this world. The author declared many years ago that his writing, as important as it is, should not be permitted to take the place of "all the other activities proper to man."

There seems to be a clue here as to why W. Somerset Maugham has not come under more critical study than he has. It is as though the critics were positive that because Maugham is not exclusively a writer he cannot be an important one. There is logic here, but it seems all bad. It is comparable to saying that because an artist does not paint everyday he cannot be a great artist. This overlooks the idea of talent. One man can work all day on a canvas, another can do better in a few minutes. W. Somerset Maugham has provided his own analogy in this work in the character of Fanny Price. There was never a more dedicated and ineffective artist.

W. Somerset Maugham has not had an easy time with his fellow novelists, either. He has taken his turn attacking them, particularly Hugh Walpole and Thomas Hardy in Cakes and Ale, and he has come in for some share of abuse too. The late German novelist Thomas Mann said that his work revealed too much of the author's own nature. Maugham thought that Mann meant he was too "superficial." Then Maugham retorted, "I am not a Mann fan."

It seems that it is too early to make a final evaluation of the talent of W. Somerset Maugham. He has proven to be very popular with the public, but some critics have placed him in a low and negative position. It seems to be the position of many avowed critics of contemporary music, painting, poetry, and literature that when an artist has found acceptance there must be something wrong. It is as though art may only be expressed by the starving artist in his garret or the frustrated novelist in his hovel. W. Somerset Maugham has confounded these critics by ignoring them. He seems to realize that the function of the creative artist is much more important than that of the critic, and that time alone will pass on the validity of his own work.

It is not an unusual situation to find that a writer has been ignored by the popular press and that he has failed to win the literary prizes of his day and yet he will prove to have a greater recognition in a succeeding generation. We might think of Herman Melville, Nathaniel Hawthorne, and Gerard Manly Hopkins in this respect. But the case of W. Somerset Maugham is quite different. He has had his popular success and he has lived extremely well on the proceeds of it. He has fulfilled his own purpose in becoming a writer. Yet he has not received the general acclaim of the literary lions of our day; it would be quite ironic and poetically appropriate if a later generation were to esteem W. Somerset Maugham in the same class with the once neglected writers mentioned above.

All great art must be measured by the ages, and perhaps we will never know the full value of the works of W. Somerset Maugham in our lifetime. We may never know the greatness of this man, as in the case of so many others, until we may look at his from the perspective of the grave. As the author once said, "Let posterity choose, I have done my work."

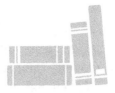

OF HUMAN BONDAGE

ESSAY QUESTIONS AND ANSWERS

. . . .

MODEL ONE

Question: Why was Philip Carey's clubfoot both a blessing and a curse in his life?

Answer: Philip Carey's clubfoot was obviously a curse to him throughout most of his life because it made him different from the other boys and men of the world. Because of the clubfoot he could not participate in athletic games or even perform the normal functions of daily living as well as others. Particularly in his youth Philip was the butt of practical jokes and meanness because he was different from the rest of the boys. It seems that many youths are quite outspoken and mean to people who have deformities. It is not that they are essentially bad people when they attack Philip; it is because they can take out their own frustration and anger on someone who is in an even more wretched situation.

And when Philip became older his clubfoot again prevented him from functioning normally. As an example he hated to hurry, to run for a train or a bus, because he was aware how ugly and silly looking his movements were. In addition, Philip developed an inferiority complex when it came to women. His terrible experience with Mildred Rogers has a scene in which he begs her to forgive him on the grounds that his clubfoot makes his life miserable. He is using the clubfoot as another type of crutch.

Even when Philip is studying to become a doctor the clubfoot is a detrimental thing. He is unable to get a position on one occasion when he desperately needs it, because the doctor to whom he applies does not think that patients would have any confidence in a doctor who is not physically perfect.

Philip's clubfoot is a blessing, too. Because he has no ability in athletics, he spends much of his time developing his mental capacities. He has much natural ability as a scholar and his appetite is stimulated by books and their magic early in life. Also, his clubfoot works as a maturing agent in Philip's life. He has suffered because of the death of his parents, but most of the suffering due to come to every person in the world is felt by Philip much earlier than usual. Since he is the point of the attack he builds up a defense to it early in life. It is a trial to go through in his youth, but it makes his adult life easier to bear.

Thus there are two sides to the coin. Philip learns to live with his deformity - he is just more obvious than those of many others. He learns to overcome much of the feeling of inadequacy due to his clubfoot, and he becomes a better person as a result.

MODEL TWO

Question: What is the reason behind Philip's rejection of Mildred after she comes to live with him?

Answer: The answer to this question is very important in relation to later developments in this novel. At this point in the book Mildred has abandoned Philip on two occasions. He has been crushed on both occasions, and somehow he has risen from his emotional defeat to begin life again. As he notes in the book, frustrated lovers seldom commit suicide. But they do suffer.

The point is that suffering has burned the love out of Philip. Suffering has matured him, and as a mature person he has a better perspective of life and life's values. This is not to say that Philip does not have some attraction for Mildred right up to the day that he proposes marriage to Sally, but it is a case of the body being dominated by the mind.

Philip wants his relationship with Mildred at this time to be friendly only. His love for her has changed in kind if not in degree. However, he is unable to see that this type of relationship is exactly what will stimulate Mildred's desires for him. In offering to help Mildred from her poverty he is putting her into a different sort of agony. He is well-intentioned, but with Mildred intentions are distorted quite easily, and she turns his kindness into a shambles.

In many respects it is through his ability to reject Mildred and his feelings for her that Philip Carey becomes a man. There are other factors undoubtedly, but when he demonstrates this control over his emotions he is functioning like a man instead of a love-struck boy. He has realized that his love was distorted all along, and it is only after he has been burned twice that he can become strong enough not to go near the fire again.

MODEL THREE

Question: In what way does W. Somerset Maugham contrast the personality of Hayward and Norah Nesbit?

Answer: There is little similarity between Hayward and Norah Nesbit. What one represents the other balances with or contrasts, and the positive side is generally in the favor of Norah. They are opposites in so many ways: in social background; in education; in determination; and particularly in a realization of their own role in the world. In this latter regard the reader should realize that for most of the novel Hayward does not know where he is going and he has no purpose in going there. He is maintained by some financial aid from his family, and he is ever elevated by the thoughts of what he is going to do with his talents. At least this enthusiasm for his own ability carries him through his youth, but a more sobering attitude comes later when he realizes along with everyone else that he has wasted his opportunities and allowed his talent to be wasted. A recognition of this would stimulate many men to make at least one great effort to prove themselves to the world, but for the present it simply turns Hayward deeper into his ego and he resorts to lies and vague references to forthcoming novels which will win him everlasting fame as a great writer. In this manner his life becomes an example of futility, and it is only by a herculean effort that he is able to put off his lethargy and don the uniform of his country to fight for its cause.

Such a radical change almost defies belief on the reader's part, but W. Somerset Maugham makes it believable when he presents it as an act of sacrifice. Even a person as confused as Hayward can come to life in dying for a noble cause. As such he performs his most important part in *Of Human Bondage*.

Norah Nesbit, on the other hand, is a person who has worked hard to fulfill her limited abilities, and she has no delusions of being remembered as a great writer even though she has been able to get into print regularly. She is the type of person who tries to accept things as they come, and though this is hard at times, she has a certain resiliency which allows her to bounce back from her troubles. Norah is not a model of Victorian virtue and in many ways she has problems which are equally as difficult as Hayward's. She becomes Philip Carey's mistress, and she loves him dearly, but she loses him when Mildred Rogers makes one of her periodic returns into the plot. It is difficult for her to accept Philip's rejection of her in favor of Mildred, especially when she knows that the other woman will be so detrimental to Philip. Yet she accepts it with as few tears as possible. The hurt is there, but it can be borne. Life will go on.

This latter point of continuing against odds shows the determination of Norah, and it contrasts with the weakness of Hayward's will. She will fight bravely in the uneven contest of man against society, but he will not even enter the arena, except to die. Yes, his death as a martyr does have its value, but W. Somerset Maugham seems to value the wisdom of Norah in eking out some small victory and at least staying alive. Incidentally, the reader might make a similar point of comparison and contrast between Norah and Fanny Price, who both loved Philip Carey, and who both lost him. Fanny's sense of values and suicide contrast sharply with Norah's determination to meet life on its own values and to live.

MODEL FOUR

Question: In what way do Thorpe Athelny and Uncle William represent conflicting values of society?

Answer: Philip Carey's Uncle William is a man of the Church, a pillar of society, a family man who has been married to the same woman for many years. He obeys the laws and pays his taxes. He is also a fraud and a hypocrite. Thorpe Athelny is a man without a church, on the lower level of society, and though he has had nine children with the same woman they are not married in the eyes of society. He too obeys the laws - more out of necessity than desire - and he pays his meager taxes with disdain. He is honest to his own code and hates religious hypocrisy.

These basic distinctions between Philip Carey's uncle and his friend point out the conflicting set of values which Philip finds thrust upon him as he travels through life. Of course the uncle was there first and for a while he made the greatest impression. But long before he went away to Paris or London Philip realized that there was much more to proper living than the lip service which his uncle gave. He had seen his uncle mock his neighbor on Saturday and get up in his pulpit on Sunday and preach brotherly love. On the other hand Athelny practiced brotherly love, both in the way he befriended the lonely Philip at first and then saved him from suicide later. Certainly this example of financial need presents the distinction in the two men, for when Philip was destitute and starving Uncle William refused to give him any money, almost gloating in the idea of "I told you so." Athelny, in contrast, went to the aid of his friend, paid his bills, took him into his home, and helped him to get a job. It would be ridiculous to ask who was the truly good man.

Another point of contrast concerning these two would be in each man's relationship to his wife. The vicar dominated his wife and always took the better part of everything, from Sunday chicken to the practice of heating a room while he was in it.

Athelny was not perfect in this respect, and there is no doubt that his wife worked harder and longer than he, but there was a sharing of things when they had them, a certain feeling of warmth which pervaded their relationship which was not found in the vicar and Aunt Louisa.

Lastly, there was a marked contrast in the intellectual climate which surrounded the vicar and Thorpe Athelny. Uncle William was a man who wore his culture and education on his sleeve, but his tastes were limited and they were circumscribed by the past. He hardly understood Philip's desire to become an artist and he discouraged him. Gentlemen simply were not involved in such a life in Paris. Athelny was certainly the opposite in virtually all of these considerations. He had received a good education and his interest in affairs of the mind continued beyond the classroom. An example of this was his interest in the paintings of El Greco. Athelny was willing to discover something new and his mind was fertile. Uncle William avoided new ideas and was content to languish in the past.

ESSAY QUESTIONS

Why did Philip Carey believe that his Uncle William was a religious hypocrite? What are the circumstances of the uncle's life which would support this view?

Why does Aunt Louisa consistently loose at chess and checkers to her husband? How does this show her goodness? Was this deception necessary in their marriage?

Why does Philip Carey turn against his friend Rose while at school? Is his reason grave enough to make them enemies?

Why does Mr. Perkins, the headmaster, allow Philip to leave school to go to Europe? Is this consistent with the teacher's ideal of education?

Why does Philip Carey defend Hayward so vigorously against the logic of Weeks when they are living in Germany? What purpose does Weeks serve in the continuity of the novel?

What were the factors which drove Fanny Price to suicide? Does Mr. Maugham agree with her way out of her problems?

What are the means which the author uses to give the reader an accurate picture of Fanny's brother Albert? What are some of the negative points which Albert represents?

How does Philip's career in Paris make him a better person?

What does Philip Carey mean by his reference to "Follow your inclinations with due regard to the policeman around the corner?" Is this a philosophy which satisfies him throughout his life?

Why was Philip Carey anxious to have Mildred Rogers fired from her job as a waitress when he first met her?

Why did Norah Nesbit consider herself a "hack-writer?" How does this reflect the author's view of literature?

What is the **irony** regarding Mildred Rogers being so fond of writings of Courtenay Paget (Norah Nesbit)?

Why was Philip Carey so determined not to see his friend Griffiths before the latter went away with Mildred? Is the same answer applicable to the reason why he refused to see Grifflths later?

Why does Philip lose his admiration for Hayward after he has been his friend for so many years? Is Philip to blame for this also?

Why does Philip feel affection for Hayward after the latter's enlistment in the army?

How was Philip influenced by the secret of the poet Cronshaw's mystery regarding the Persian rug? Was this influence lasting?

What is the background of Thorpe Athelny which makes him such a memorable person? How does Athelny influence Philip's life?

Why does Philip find such an attraction to the painting of El Greco and to the culture of Spain? Is this a valid point of attraction?

How is the death of Hayward in many ways the fulfillment of his life? Would this same answer also apply to Cronshaw?

How does the relationship between Thorpe Athelny and his common-law wife reflect W. Somerset Maugham's attitude toward accepted social values?

Why does Philip Carey avoid the painter Lawson at the end of the novel after he has been friendly with him for so many years?

Why is Philip Carey safe at night as a doctor in the most savage slums in London. What does this show about the basic dignity of mankind?

Why does Philip Carey stay with Sally Athelny after he realizes that he does not have to marry her? Is this an important revelation to the reader as well as to Philip himself?

In what circumstances are Sally and Mildred similar? In what ways are they different?

What is the over-all point of view of W. Somerset Maugham in *Of Human Bondage*? Do you think that this novel accomplishes what the author set out to do?

BIBLIOGRAPHY

Allen, Walter. *The English Novel*. E. P. Dutton and Co., New York,

Brander, L. *Somerset Maugham: A Guide. Oliver and Boyd, Lt'd.*, London, 1963.

Cordell, Richard A. *W. Somerset Maugham*. Thomas Nelson and Sons, Toronto and New York, 1937.

Jonas, Klaus W. *The Maugham Enigma: An Anthology*. The Citadel Press, New York, 1954. (This is valuable for the student of Maugham, for it contains a number of critical essays, many by well-known writers, scholars, and critics, and is the only convenient collection of such writings about Maugham).

Pfeiffer, Karl G. *W. Somerset Maugham: A Candid Portrait*. W. W. Norton and Co., New York. 1958.

Wagenknecht, Edward. *Cavalcade of the English Novel*. Holt, Rinehart, and Winston, New York.

CPSIA information can be obtained
at www.ICGtesting.com
Printed in the USA
LVHW080535280421
685801LV00015B/1305